MS-Office 97
explained

BOOKS AVAILABLE

MS-Office 97
explained

by

N. Kantaris
and
P.R.M. Oliver

BERNARD BABANI (publishing) LTD
THE GRAMPIANS
SHEPHERDS BUSH ROAD
LONDON W6 7NF
ENGLAND

PLEASE NOTE

Although every care has been taken with the production of this book to ensure that any projects, designs, modifications and/or programs, etc., contained herewith, operate in a correct and safe manner and also that any components specified are normally available in Great Britain, the Publishers and Author(s) do not accept responsibility in any way for the failure (including fault in design) of any project, design, modification or program to work correctly or to cause damage to any equipment that it may be connected to or used in conjunction with, or in respect of any other damage or injury that may be so caused, nor do the Publishers accept responsibility in any way for the failure to obtain specified components.

Notice is also given that if equipment that is still under warranty is modified in any way or used or connected with home-built equipment then that warranty may be void.

© 1997 BERNARD BABANI (publishing) LTD

First Published – June 1997
Reprinted – June 1998

British Library Cataloguing in Publication Data:

A catalogue record for this book is available from the British Library

ISBN 0 85934 426 6

Cover Design by Gregor Arthur
Cover illustration by Adam Willis
Printed and Bound in Great Britain by Cox & Wyman Ltd, Reading

ABOUT THIS BOOK

MS Office 97 explained has been written to help users to get to grips with the integrated components of this package, namely, the word processor *Word 97*, the spreadsheet *Excel 97*, the presentation graphics *PowerPoint 97*, and the new desktop manager *Outlook 97*. If you have *MS Office 97 Pro*, the package should also include the database *Access 97*, which is also covered in this book. All these components were specifically designed for the *Windows 95,* and *NT* environments.

The book does not describe how to install and use Microsoft Windows. If you need to know more about Windows, then may we suggest you select an appropriate level book for your needs from the 'Books Available' list - the books are loosely graduated in complexity with the less demanding *One step at a time* series, to the more detailed *Explained* series. They are all published by BERNARD BABANI (publishing) Ltd.

The individual applications which make up Microsoft Office 97 are designed to work together and have the same look and feel, which makes it easy to learn. For example, the majority of menus, toolbar buttons, and dialogue boxes are the same in each application, which gives them a consistent interface, and makes it easier to share information between them.

The package improves on previous Office capabilities, such as the ability to

- create and edit hyperlinks from within any of its applications to any Office document, HTML file, or any file on internal or external Web or FTP sites,

- use browser-style query techniques to search text in both HTML and Office documents on local networks and the Internet,

- share documents with other users within a company's network.

Below we list some of the new features to this latest version of Microsoft Office:

- The Office Assistant; an online, natural language interface to assist you with the tasks in hand.

- Command Bars; an enhanced user interface which provides a unified system of toolbars and menus across all applications of Office 97.

- Office Tools which gives a consistent interface to a number of graphics and drawing facilities across Word, Excel, and PowerPoint.

- The addition of Outlook 97, specifically designed to help users manage e-mail, contact lists, calendars, to do lists, and documents.

- Improved IntelliSense features which help you with your work, no matter which application you are using.

The various applications within Microsoft Office 97 can either be used by themselves or made to share information. This book introduces each application by itself, with sufficient detail to get you working, then discusses how to share information between them. No prior knowledge of these packages is assumed.

The book was written with the busy person in mind. It is not necessary to learn all there is to know about a subject, when reading a few selected pages can usually do the same thing quite adequately. With the help of this book, it is hoped that you will be able to come to terms with Microsoft Office and get the most out of your computer in terms of efficiency, productivity and enjoyment, and that you will be able to do it in the shortest, most effective and informative way.

If you would like to purchase a Companion Disc for any of the listed books by the same author(s), apart from the ones marked with an asterisk, containing the file/program listings which appear in them, then fill in the form at the back of the book and send it to Phil Oliver at the stipulated address.

ABOUT THE AUTHORS

Noel Kantaris graduated in Electrical Engineering at Bristol University and after spending three years in the Electronics Industry in London, took up a Tutorship in Physics at the University of Queensland. Research interests in Ionospheric Physics, led to the degrees of M.E. in Electronics and Ph.D. in Physics. On return to the UK, he took up a Post-Doctoral Research Fellowship in Radio Physics at the University of Leicester, and then in 1973 a lecturing position in Engineering at the Camborne School of Mines, Cornwall, (part of Exeter University), where since 1978 he has also assumed the responsibility for the Computing Department.

Phil Oliver graduated in Mining Engineering at Camborne School of Mines in 1967 and since then has specialised in most aspects of surface mining technology, with a particular emphasis on computer related techniques. He has worked in Guyana, Canada, several Middle Eastern countries, South Africa and the United Kingdom, on such diverse projects as: the planning and management of bauxite, iron, gold and coal mines; rock excavation contracting in the UK; international mining equipment sales and international mine consulting for a major mining house in South Africa. In 1988 he took up a lecturing position at Camborne School of Mines (part of Exeter University) in Surface Mining and Management.

ACKNOWLEDGEMENTS

We would like to thank the staff of Text 100 Limited for providing the software programs on which this work was based. We would also like to thank colleagues at the Camborne School of Mines for the helpful tips and suggestions which assisted us in the writing of this book.

TRADEMARKS

CONTENTS

1. PACKAGE OVERVIEW

Microsoft Office 97 is a collection of powerful, full-featured, programs with the same look and feel that work together as if they were a single program. Office 97 was specifically designed to allow you to work with your information data, either by yourself or to share such data with others, if you so wish, quickly and efficiently.

Microsoft Office 97 Standard edition includes MS-Word, MS-Excel, and MS-PowerPoint. The Professional edition also includes the fully relational database management system MS-Access. With both editions of Office 97 you also get MS-Outlook, a desktop information and time manager. All Office 97 applications have a built-in consistency which makes them easier to use. For example, they all have standardised toolbars and consistent menus, commands, and dialogue boxes. Once you become familiar with one application, it is far easier to learn and use the others.

MS-Office 97 applications are the most integrated to date. Just like its predecessor, Office 97 applications make use of what is known as IntelliSense, which anticipates what you want to do and produces the correct result. For example, AutoCorrect, AutoFormat, and AutoComplete in Word can, when activated, automatically correct common spelling mistakes, format an entire document, or complete the word you are typing.

Other common code, first introduced in Office 95, is: The Office Binder which allows you to group all your documents, workbooks, and presentations for a project in one place. Microsoft Visual Basic for Applications, which gives you a powerful and flexible development platform with which to create custom solutions. The Wizards in all Office 97 applications which can help you with everyday tasks and/or simplify complex tasks.

Office 97 comes with a lot more common code between applications, adding the following facilities:

- Command Bars - designed to unify all the toolbars and menus for all applications in the Office 97 suite. Command bars can be highly customised, allowing you, for example, to move selected drop-down menus anywhere in the application workspace for easy access.

- Office Assistant - an animated online help which is the central source of information in each application. This replaces the Answer Wizard, Tip Wizard, and Help menus in Office 95. In addition, the Office Assistant can be programmed to assist with Office based custom-built applications by, for example, taking a user step-by-step through a given procedure.

- Office Tools - provides a consistent interface to a range of graphics and drawing tools across Word, Excel and PowerPoint. Tools such as Drawing, WordArt, and Picture, to name but a few, are common to all three applications. Other tools provide application specific features, such as extended charting options in Excel.

- Object Linking and Embedding (OLE) - can be used to move and share information seamlessly between Office 97 applications. For example, you can drag information from one application to another, or you can link information from one application into another.

- Hyperlinks - can be used from any of the Office 97 applications to access a common dialogue box which allows you to build or edit hyperlinks to other Office documents, to any file on an internal or external Web or FTP (File Transfer Protocol) site, or to HTML (Hypertext Markup Language) files. This helps you use your documents with the Internet.

Hardware and Software Requirements

If Microsoft Office is already installed on your computer, you can safely skip this and the next section of this chapter.

To install and use MS Office, you need an IBM-compatible PC equipped with Intel's 80486 (or higher) processor. In addition, you need the following:

- Windows 95, Windows NT or Windows NT Advanced Server version.

- Random access memory (RAM): 8MB; 16MB recommended when running multiple programs.

- Hard disc space available for MS Office 97 Standard: 61MB for typical; 131MB for custom. For MS Office 97 Professional: 121MB for typical; 191MB for custom; 60 MB for running it from a CD-ROM.

- Video adapter: VGA or higher resolution. If you are using PowerPoint, you will need a 256-colour video adapter.

- Pointing device: Microsoft Mouse or compatible.

Realistically, to run MS Office 97 Pro with reasonable sized applications, you will need a Pentium PC with at least 16MB of RAM. To run Microsoft Office 97 from a network, you must also have a network compatible with your Windows operating environment, such as Microsoft's Windows 95, Windows NT, LAN Manager, or Novell's NetWare.

Finally, if you are connected to the Internet, you can take advantage of Word's advanced editing and formatting features when working with e-mail messages. To use Word as your e-mail editor, you must have Microsoft Outlook or Microsoft Exchange installed on your computer and in that program have Word 97 selected as your e-mail editor.

Installing MS Office 97

Installing MS Office on your computer's hard disc is made very easy with the use of the SETUP program, which even configures MS Office automatically to take advantage of the computer's hardware. One of SETUP's functions is to convert compressed Office files from the distribution discs, or CD-ROM, prior to copying them onto your hard disc.

Note: If you are using a virus detection utility, disable it before running SETUP, as it might conflict with it.

To install MS Office, click the **Start** button and select the **Run** command, as shown below left. Selecting this command, opens the Run dialogue box, as shown below right.

If the application was distributed on diskettes, insert disc #1 into the A: drive and type in the **Command Line** box:

```
a:\setup
```

In our case we used the CD-ROM in the F: drive. Clicking the **OK** button, starts the installation of Microsoft Office 97. SETUP displays the following screen:

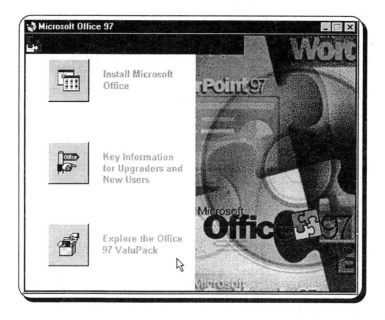

We suggest that you first look at the 'Key information for Upgragraders and New Users' before proceeding with the installation.

Clicking the 'Install Microsoft Office' button, causes SETUP to do the following:

- Asks you to close any open applications.

- Searches your system's discs for installed Office components.

- Prompts you to type your name and the name of your organisation (optional).

- Prompts you to write down the product ID number on your registration card.

- Prompts you to supply the path to the directory where you want to install Office, and then checks your system and the available hard disc space.

Next, select the type of installation you want. The SETUP program provides three basic options. The available options vary depending on how you are installing Office; directly from discs or CD-ROM.

 Typical installs all Office applications and popular components. This installation (it requires 121 MB for the Professional version), is recommended for most users.

 Custom includes **Typical** and the option to add or remove components. This installation (it requires 191 MB for the Professional version), is recommended for power users.

 Run from CD-ROM is only available if you are setting up Office 97 from a CD-ROM (it requires 60 MB for the Professional version). Shared components are installed on the hard disc.

If you select the **Custom** installation, the following dialogue box is displayed:

Microsoft Office 97 - Maintenance		? X

In the Options list, select the items you want installed; clear the items you want to be removed.

A grayed box with a check indicates that only part of the component will be installed. To select all components in the Option list, click Select All.

Options:

		Description:
☑ Microsoft Binder	1702 K	Microsoft Binder will be installed with only the selected options.
☑ Microsoft Excel	31163 K	
☑ Microsoft Word	32743 K	
☑ Microsoft PowerPoint	31465 K	
☑ Microsoft Access	49963 K	
☑ Microsoft Outlook	28569 K	
☑ Web Page Authoring (HTML)	7794 K	
☑ Microsoft Bookshelf Basics	161 K	
☑ Data Access	10223 K	Change Option...
☑ Office Tools	17847 K	Select All

Folder for Currently Selected Option:

D:\msoffice\Office   Change Folder...

Space required on D:	128400 K	Components to Add:	0
Space available on D:	67040 K	Components to Remove:	0

Continue   Cancel

6

Make sure the check boxes next to the application or component names are selected for all items that you want to install. A selected item displays a "√" in its check box. If you do not want to install an application or component, make sure that its check box is cleared by clicking it. To install all of the applications and all of their components, choose the **Continue** button.

To install part of an application or component, highlight its name by clicking it, then click the **Change Option** button. Clear the check boxes for any options you don't want to install, and then choose the **OK** button. When you finish, choose the **Continue** button. Depending on the options you select, you may need to respond to additional prompts.

SETUP creates a list of previous Office files, including the Office Shortcut Bar, then asks you to select the paper format and language you are using, before proceeding with the installation. If SETUP detects the presence of Schedule+ 95 on your machine, it will ask you whether you would prefer to use it as your primary calendar instead of Outlook.

Finally, SETUP removes all unecessary files of a previous Office installation from your system's hard disc, before starting to transfer the new Office 97 files to it, as shown below.

 Throughout installation SETUP informs you on what it is doing and what percentage of the total file transfer it has covered, as shown here. It then removes all duplicate files from your system and informs you if the installation is completed successfully.

7

The Office Shortcut Bar

During installation, the Office Shortcut Bar is collated and added to the Windows Start Up program so that it will be displayed automatically on your screen whenever you start your PC. The contents of a Microsoft Shortcut Bar used with a previous version of Office will be preserved. The Shortcut Bar will be displayed when you restart your computer.

The Microsoft Office Shortcut Bar, provides a convenient way to work with your documents and the Office applications by complementing the Windows **Start** menu.

The various icons on the Shortcut Bar, shown here, have the following function:

Getting Results Book

New Office Document

Open Office Document

Microsoft Bookshelf Basics

New Note

New Message

New Journal Entry

Microsoft Outlook

New Appointment

New Task

New Contact

The first icon of the above Office Toolbar (Getting Results Book) is only available to you if you are connected to a company's network or the Internet and have installed a browser, such as Microsoft's Explorer, or Netscape. This option allows you to use browser-style query techniques on both HTML and Office documents on an internal network or the Internet.

8

The function of other icons on the toolbar is as follows:

The New Office Document button: Allows you to select in the displayed dialogue box the tab containing the type of document you want to work with. Double-clicking the type of document or template you want, automatically loads the appropriate application.

The Open Office Document button: Allows you to work with an existing document. Opening a document, first starts the application originally used to create it.

The Microsoft Bookshelf Basics: Allows a preview of the world of information found in the complete version of the Bookshelf which provides access to three major reference books; *The American Heritage Dictionary*, *The Original Roget's Thesaurus*, and *The Columbia Dictionary of Quotations*. This facility requires you to have a CD-ROM.

The New buttons: Allow you to make a New Note, a New Message, or a New Journal Entry to schedule your time effectively.

The Microsoft Outlook button: Activates the Office 97 new desktop manager used to manage your e-mail, contact lists, tasks and documents.

The New Appointment button: Allows you to add a new appointment in your management system. This caters for all-day or multiple-day events and a meeting planner, including meeting request processing and attendance lists.

The New Task button: Allows you to add a new task in your management system, including automatic composition of an e-mail message summarising a task and automatic tracking of tasks sent to other users.

The New Contact button: Allows you to enter a new contact in Outlook's database, or to send an e-mail message direct from the contact manager and use hyperlinks for direct access to a contact's home page on the Internet.

Adding or Removing Office Applications:

To add or remove an Office application

- Close all open applications, including the Office Shortcut Bar. To do the latter, left-click the area with the small button at the top of the Office Shortcut Bar, shown here, then click the **Exit** option.

- Point to **Settings** on the Windows **Start** menu, and click Control Panel. Next, double-click the Add/Remove Programs icon, shown here, and then click the Install/Uninstall tab. Click the Microsoft Office application, and then click **Add/Remove**.

  Add/Rem...
  Programs

- Follow the instructions on the screen.

To recover the Office Shortcut Bar, click **Start**, select **Find, Files or Folders**, and type *Shortcut* in the **Named** box. In our case, double-clicking the second of the two found files, restores the Office Shortcut Bar.

Name	In Folder	Size	Type
Shortcut to Northw...	C:\My Documents	1KB	Shortcut
Microsoft Office S...	C:\WINDOWS\Start...	1KB	Shortcut

Alternatively, you could wait for the automatic recovery and display of the Shortcut Bar which will take place next time you switch on your computer and Windows is loaded.

Changing the Office Shortcut Bar:

You have the option of changing the buttons on the Office Shortcut Bar. To do so, left-click on an empty part of the Shortcut bar to display the available options, as shown at the bottom below.

Of these, we find the 'Programs' option the most useful. Clicking this option, replaces the original Office Shortcut Bar with the one shown here. However, clicking the Office icon (top left), changes the Shortcut Bar back to the original Office and places the Old Office icon (bottom left) at the extreme bottom of the Bar. You can then flick between the two by clicking the appropriate icon. The function of the various buttons on the Old Office Shortcut Bar are as shown on the right.

Adding/Deleting Buttons:

You can add buttons to the Shortcut Bar by dragging them there. To find the application you want to add to the Shortcut Bar, click the **Start** button and use **Find**.

To delete a button, right-click on an empty part of the Shortcut Bar, select **Customize** from the displayed menu, then click the Buttons tab, select the unwanted button and click **Delete**. But beware, this also deletes the folder that holds the application! It may be better to hide it.

Hiding/Displaying Buttons:

To hide a button from the Shortcut Bar (without deleting it), right-click on the button and select the **Hide Button** option on the displayed menu, shown here.

To display previously hidden buttons, right-click the Shortcut Bar, use the **Customize** option on the displayed menu and click the Button tab. Clicking on the check box of the required button makes it visible on the Shortcut Bar. Clicking again, clears its check mark and hides it.

The Mouse Pointers

In MS Office applications, as with all other graphical based programs, the use of a mouse makes many operations both easier and more fun to carry out.

MS Office makes use of the mouse pointers available in Windows, some of the most common of which are illustrated below. When an MS Office application is initially started up the first you will see is the hourglass, which turns into an upward pointing hollow arrow once the individual application screen appears on your display. Other shapes depend on the type of work you are doing at the time.

  The hourglass which displays when you are waiting while performing a function.

The arrow which appears when the pointer is placed over menus, scrolling bars, and buttons.

The I-beam which appears in normal text areas of the screen.

12

✛ The large 4-headed arrow which appears after choosing the **Control, Move/Size** command(s) for moving or sizing windows.

↔ The double arrows which appear when over the border of a window, used to drag the side and alter the size of the window.

🖑 The Help hand which appears in the Help windows, and is used to access 'hypertext' type links.

MS Office applications, like other Windows packages, have additional mouse pointers which facilitate the execution of selected commands. Some of these are:

↓ The vertical pointer which appears when pointing over a column in a table or worksheet and used to select the column.

➡ The horizontal pointer which appears when pointing at a row in a table or worksheet and used to select the row.

↖ The slanted arrow which appears when the pointer is placed in the selection bar area of text or a table.

◀╫▶ The vertical split arrow which appears when pointing over the area separating two columns and used to size a column.

⬍ The horizontal split arrow which appears when pointing over the area separating two rows and used to size a row.

+ The frame cross which you drag to create a frame.

✐ The draw pointer which appears when you are drawing freehand.

Using the Office Assistant

The Office Assistant is a central source of application information. No matter which Office 97 application you are using, the Assistant is there to help you.

To find out how it works, click the Office Assistant button, shown here, with the left mouse button, type the word **help** in the displayed 'What would you like to do?' box, shown to the left, and left-click the **Search** button.

A list of help topics is then displayed, as shown to the right. To see more topics, left-click the small triangle at the bottom of the list. To find out how you can use the Office Assistant, click the 'Ways to get assistance while you work' option which causes the display of the screen shown on the next page. From this latter screen you can find out all there is to know about the Office Assistant.

The very same screen can be displayed from all Office applications, with only the title of the window changing to reflect the application in use.

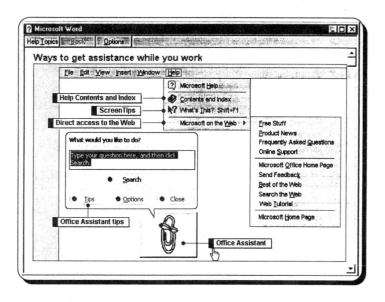

Ways to get assistance while you work

Clicking the left mouse button on areas of the screen
that causes the mouse pointer to change to a pointing
hand (there are five such areas), displays additional
information on the selected topic. The changed pointer
is shown at the bottom of the above screen dump.

Customising the Office Assistant:

You can customise the Office Assistant to a great
degree. Not only can you change the way it responds
to your enquiries, but you can even switch it off once
you have mastered a particular Office application.

To see the default options
settings of the Office Assistant,
activate it, left-click on it, and
left-click the **Options** button on
the displayed box, shown here.

Doing this, causes the
following dialogue box to be
displayed on your screen:

15

As you can see, it is possible to choose from several options. Should you like to change the shape of your Office Assistant (there are nine shapes to choose from - see next page), either left-click the Gallery tab of the above dialogue box, or right-click the Office Assistant and select the **Choose Assistant** option from the displayed menu, as shown below.

Either action displays the following dialogue box in which you can select your preferred Assistant shape by left-clicking the **Next** button.

The shapes of the available Assistants are as follows:

Using the Help Menu

Another way of getting help in an Office application is to left-click the **Help** menu option at the top of the application window, and select the **Contents and Index** option of the displayed sub-menu, shown here. This displays the Contents dialogue box, shown below.

You can either view information on the screen or print it on paper. Left-clicking the Find tab, displays a dialogue box with three areas for typing, selecting and displaying information, as shown below.

Typing, for example, the words **find fast** in the first 'Find' box, causes a list of related topics to appear automatically in the second 'Select' box. Selection of one or more matching words from the displayed list narrows down the selection of topics appearing in the third 'Display' box.

Finally, selecting a topic from the third display box by left-clicking it to highlight it and pressing the **Display** button at the bottom of the dialogue box, produces information on your selection.

If the topic you want to select is not visible within the display area of the third box, use the scroll bar to get to it.

As an exercise, click the Index tab of the Help Topics dialogue box and type the word 'open' in the first text box. Immediately the topic 'Opening documents' appears in the second text box, as shown below.

Next, double-click on the selected item to display all you need to know, in this instance, about the Word 97, 95, and 6.0 file formats. Similar searches carried out from other Office 97 applications will reveal what you should do if you require backward compatibility.

It is worth while exploring the different ways in which you can get help with or without the Office Assistant. For example, you can implement the **F1** function key to give you context sensitive help whenever you press it. To find out how to do this, select the 'Getting help without the Office Assistant' option in the 'What would you like to do?' list (see page 14).

Another way of getting context sensitive help is to select the **'What's This'** option from the **Help** sub-menu, then move the modified mouse pointer to an area of the document, or onto a particular Toolbar button, and press the left mouse button.

2. MICROSOFT OUTLOOK 97

Microsoft's Outlook 97 is a new desktop information manager that offers a lot more than Schedule+, which appeared as an added extra with Office 95. Outlook 97 can be made the centre of activity for all the other Office 97 applications. It can be used *online* or *offline*.

To work online, your computer must be connected to a shared network resource, which is imperative if you are planning to use Outlook's group-scheduling features. In that case, your computer must have a connection to a *postoffice* which is a list of Mail users on the system. Outlook 97 can do the following:

- Manage information such as your appointments, contacts, tasks, and files, and if your computer is connected to a network, manage your e-mail, use group scheduling, and public folders.

- Share information with other Office programs, and browse and find Office files from within Outlook.

- Share information across the World Wide Web, provided you are connected to the Internet and have a browser, such as Netscape or Microsoft's Explorer. To install the latter, double-click on the 'Setup for Microsoft Internet Explorer' icon on your desktop, placed there by the Office 97 installation program.

The two major examples of integration of Outlook 97 with the rest of the Office suite are TaskLinks, which enable users to add to the Outlook's list of tasks from within any of the other Office 97 applications, and the Journal, which automatically tracks use of the other Office applications. The latter can be customised to monitor as many or as few entries of activity as required, for example, to record an entry every time you open, save or print a document from any of Office 97's applications. The result can be a time map of the user's day's or week's activity.

Starting Microsoft Outlook 97

Outlook 97 is started in Windows either by clicking the
 Start button then selecting **Program** and
clicking on the 'Microsoft Outlook 97' icon on
the cascade menu, or by clicking any of the
six icons 'New Message', 'New Journal Entry'
'Microsoft Outlook', 'New Appointment', 'New
Task', or 'New Contact' on the Office
Shortcut Bar, or by clicking the 'Open Office
Document' icon on the Office Shortcut Bar
and double-clicking on an Outlook file. In the
latter case the schedule file will be loaded
into Outlook 97 at the same time.

If you have both Outlook 97 and
Schedule+ on your computer, provided you
have selected this option during installation,
then clicking the Schedule+ icon on the
Office Shortcut Bar will activate the
Schedule+ program. Whether you have
selected to keep Schedule+ or not, Outlook
97 can convert all your Schedule+ calendar
and schedule files into Outlook 97 format, but having
done so, converted files can not be read by Schedule+.

When you start Outlook 97 the program momentarily
displays its opening screen, shown below, and then
displays the Inbox screen shown on the next page.

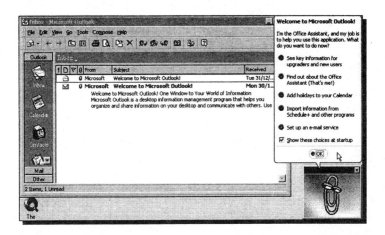

We suggest that you spend some time looking at all the items on the Help List, starting with the 'See key information for upgraders and new users', which will display additional topics on the screen as follows:

Managing Information

You can use Outlook to effectively manage information whether it is personal or business. The Inbox screen provides you with the means to manage information on three general topics: Outlook, Mail, and Other.

The Outlook option provides the following tools:

Inbox - used to send and receive messages, preview messages before you open them, and use Message Flags to mark them with a follow-up action.

Calendar - used to keep track of your schedule and plan meetings with others. Use the TaskPad to see the day's tasks.

Contacts - used to keep your personal and business contact information up-to-date. Sort and file contacts any way you want, and go directly to their Web page.

Tasks - used to organise your personal and business to-do list in one easy-to-manage place.

Journal - used to record Outlook items, such as e-mail messages and files that are important, and to record and track activities of all types.

Notes - used to write down notes on anything you like, or drop text in notes that you want to re-use in other places.

Recycle bin - used to find deleted items and reinstate them.

Mail provides the following tools:

Inbox - used to send and receive messages, preview messages before you open them, etc.

Sent Items - used to manage mail you have sent to others, a copy of which is saved in the sent items folder. Items can be sorted in any way you like.

Outbox - used to configure the way you send messages by delaying their delivery, or make them unavailable after a specified date.

Recycle bin - used to find deleted items and reinstate them.

Other provides the following tools:

My Computer - used to search drives and folders for a file you want to view, use, or perform housekeeping operations on such as delete it or rename it.

My Documents - used to store Office documents, worksheets, databases, and presentations that you are working on inside the same folder.

Favorites - used to insert shortcuts to frequently used folders.

In general, you can use Outlook to open, view, and share other Office program files and use its various tools to help you work more efficiently.

Parts of the Outlook Screen

Before we go any further, let us take a look at the Outlook opening screen.

As you can see, there are several symbols which display on the Outlook screen. To find out what they are (they are too numerous to list here), highlight an item on the Inbox list and left-click the Assistant icon shown to the left, to display the help screen shown to the right. To see the list of symbols, left-click the first item on the Assistant's list. Try it, you need to know what they are.

26

The Inbox Toolbar

Apart from the symbols that appear on the screen of the various Outlook options, the icons on the Toolbar also change from one option to the other.

Below, we show the Inbox toolbar icons with an explanation of their function.

New Mail Message. Click the arrow to get ⇩

Back

Forward

Up one Level

Folder List

Print

Print Preview

Move to Folder

Delete

Reply

Reply to All

Forward

Address Book

Find Items

Office Assistant

Mail Message	Ctrl+N
Post in This Folder	Ctrl+Shift+S
Appointment	Ctrl+Shift+A
Meeting Request	Ctrl+Shift+Q
Contact	Ctrl+Shift+C
Task	Ctrl+Shift+K
Task Request	Ctrl+Shift+U
Journal Entry	Ctrl+Shift+J
Note	Ctrl+Shift+N
Office Document	Ctrl+Shift+H
Choose Template...	
Choose Form...	
Folder...	Ctrl+Shift+E

Pointing to an icon and clicking the left mouse button can display a drop-down menu, as shown above right, action a command, such as displaying the Folder List, or open an appropriate dialogue box so that you can, for example, access the address book or search for items, such as folders or files.

Importing Information

If you already hold personal or business information, such as contacts or tasks to perform, on either Schedule+ or another program, now is the time to import these into Outlook.

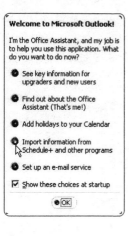

The Assistant's help screen to the right is opened automatically when you first start Outlook. To convert information, simply click the 'Import Information' button and follow the Wizard's instructions on the screen.

Below, we selected to import information from Schedule+ 7.0, our previously used scheduler.

Clicking the **Next** button, starts the process and after a short period the Import Wizard locates the old Schedule+ 7.0 files, as shown on the next page.

In our case the Wizard found three files. In your case these will most certainly be different.

To find out what we have converted, click the Find
Items icon on the Toolbar, shown here, and
select the appropriate item in the **Look for**
box. We have selected 'Tasks' and clicked the
Find Now button to display the following:

Using the Calendar

Before we start entering information in our Calendar, let us take a look at its opening screen.

Viewing Appointments:

When in Daily view, to look at another day, left-click on the day you want to look at on the monthly calendar at the top right of the screen.

To view a week or a month at once, use the **View, Week** or **View, Month** command, as shown to the left, or simply click the appropriate button on the Calendar Toolbar, shown below.

Whichever method you use the result is the same.

Clicking the monthly button, displays a typical, though almost empty, monthly diary, as shown below.

Changing the month you are viewing could not be simpler; just click the scroll buttons of the vertical scroll bar - clicking the upper scroll button displays earlier months, while clicking the lower scroll button displays later months.

All the details of appointments, events or meetings can be viewed in Outlook whether you are in the Daily, Weekly, or Monthly view; you can see the date, time, and the description. You also have the facility to use symbols to indicate whether the appointment is recurring, tentative, or private, and whether a reminder has been set, shown by a small bell, or other users have been invited (these will be discussed next).

Information relevant to an appointment or meeting is also displayed in the Appointment dialogue box. To organise a meeting, however, you will need to click the Meeting Planner tab of the dialogue box.

Scheduling an Appointment, Meeting, or Event

Before you start scheduling an appointment, meeting or event, it is necessary to look at the following definitions:

- An appointment does not involve other colleagues or resources, and can be recurring, that is, it can be repeated on a regular basis.

- A meeting is an appointment that involves other people and possibly resources, and can also be recurring.

- An event is an activity that lasts one day, or more, such as attendance at an exhibition or conference. An annual event, occurs yearly on a specific date. Events and annual events do not occupy blocks of time in your Calendar; instead, they appear as a banner below the current day heading.

Entering Appointments:

To start with, let us type in a recurring appointment to meet our Accountant, that takes place on the first Thursday of every month starting at 10:00 a.m. on 6 February and lasts for 1½ hours. To do so, click on 6 February on the calendar to the right of the entry area, move the cursor to 10:00 a.m. and click the Make a New Appointment icon, shown here. This opens the Appointment dialogue box displayed on the next page in which you can type 'Meeting Accountant' in the **Subject** box, and 'My Office' in the **Location** box, set the **End time** to 11.30, and press the **Recurrence** button on the Toolbar.

In the Appointment Recurrence dialogue box, click the **Monthly** and **The** radio buttons on either side of the displayed mouse pointer on our screen dump, and click **OK**. Finally, click the **Save and Close** button on the first dialogue box.

Meeting Accountant - Appointment

File Edit View Insert Format Tools Appointment Help

Save and Close | 🖨 | ✂ 🗐 🛍 📎 | 🕮 | 🔍 × ▲ ▾ ◆ ▾ | ❓

Recurrence

| Appointment | Meeting Planner |

Subject: Meeting Accountant

Location: My Office

Start time: Thu 06/02/97   10:00   ☐ All day event
End time: Thu 06/02/97   11:30

☑ Reminder: 15 minutes ⏰   Show time as: Busy

Categories...   Private ☐

Appointment Recurrence   ? ×

Appointment time
Start: 10:00   End: 11:30   Duration: 1.5 hours

Recurrence pattern
○ Daily   ○ Day 6 of every 1 month(s)
○ Weekly
● Monthly   ● The first Thursday of every 1 month(s)
○ Yearly

Range of recurrence
Start: Thu 06/02/1997   ● No end date
○ End after: 10 occurrences
○ End by: Thu 06/11/1997

OK   Cancel   Remove Recurrence

Your Calendar now shows the latest entry, together

🔔 Meeting Accountant (My Office)

with the Reminder icon and the Recurring symbol.

33

If you want to make any changes to the newly created appointment, point to it and right-click it. You can use the options on this drop-down menu to edit, delete, or move the appointment. Choosing the **Edit Series** option, opens the Recurrent Appointment dialogue box where you can make the required changes.

Next, let us assume that you also have a special lunch appointment with your mother on the same day, but four weeks later, as it is her birthday. To enter this information click on 6 March on the calendar to the right of the Daily entry area, and create a yearly appointment 'Lunch with mother' for 1:00 p.m., for 1½ hours, as shown below. Add as a note the reminder 'Birthday lunch'.

Note that the meeting with the Accountant is also shown on the same day, as it is four weeks since the last meeting. This information also appears on the Weekly and the Monthly view. Try it!

Printing Information:

Information held in a diary can be printed on paper. Simply use the **File, Print** command and select an appropriate item from the **Print Style** list displayed in the Print dialogue box. However, before committing anything to paper, use the **Preview** button and save a few trees! Below we show a printout of the 'Daily Style'.

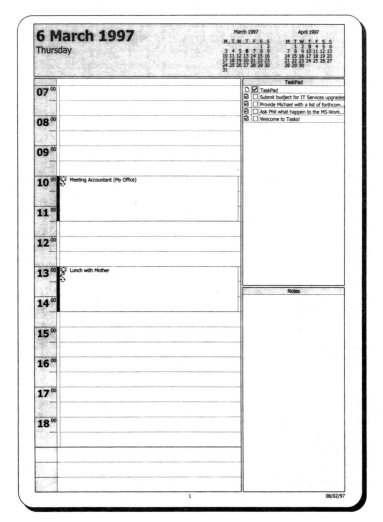

35

Planning a Meeting:

Suppose we decide to invite other people into the meeting with the Accountant on 6 March. First, locate the date of the meeting on the Appointments display and double-click the entry in question. In the displayed Assistant's 'Open Recurring Item' screen, click the 'Open this occurrence' radio button to display the Recurring Appointment dialogue box.

In this dialogue box, click the Meeting Planner tab to obtain the following screen, in which we typed the names of two colleagues we would like to be present at the meeting.

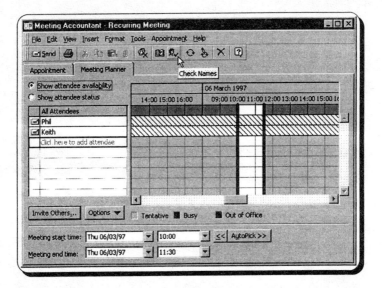

From here, you can organise meetings and send requests to participants and then track the status of their response provided, of course, you are connected to a local network. You can even give other Outlook users permissions to view your diary and to plan meetings with you at times when you are not so busy, but still be able to maintain private information in your diary.

Other Outlook Facilities

Apart from 'Appointments', Outlook contains all the other elements needed to give you an effective time-management tool. These elements are accessed by appropriate tabs situated on the left edge of the screen. Each tab includes one or more of the following:

Contacts:

The Contacts tab displays your contacts in a combined business card and list view. You can change the way information is displayed by using the **View, Current View** command. What is shown below is the Address Cards view format - you have the choice of five additional types of views.

To add a new contact, use the **Contacts, New Contact** command, which displays a multi-tab dialogue box in which you type relevant information.

Contact lists can be saved under different group names, so that you can have one list for your local company branch, and another for a different branch.

Tasks:

Tasks appear in the daily and weekly view of Calendar, or can be displayed by clicking on the Task icon of the Outlook options bar. Tasks are used to organise your personal to-do list, as well as keep track of your business. Below we show a list of personal tasks, with their due date of completion.

Tasks can be assigned to other people within your organisation, and can help you keep track of progress on work that other people do for you or in co-operation with you. For example, you might assign a task to a colleague, or a colleague might assign a task to you in a group effort.

A task assignment requires at least two people: one to send a task request and another to respond to it. When you send a task request, you give up ownership of the task, but can keep an updated copy of it in your task list and receive status reports, but you cannot change information in it. The person that receives the task request is the temporary owner of the task until acceptance of the task, in which case that person becomes the new, permanent owner of that task. Only temporary or permanent owners of a task can update that task. If a task is declined, ownership of the task is returned to the person who sent the task request.

To find out how to use the various functions appearing on a Tasks list, use the Help Assistant and search for 'tasks'. On the displayed list, click the Tasks radio button to obtain the following screen.

Using Help in this way, you will learn quickly how to sort and give priority to tasks, track task progress, enter recurring tasks once, assign tasks to others, and keep complex task lists organised.

Journal:

The following activities can be automatically recorded in Journal.

- E-mail messages
- Meeting requests
- Meeting responses
- Task requests
- Task responses

Clicking the Journal icon on the Outlook options bar, displays the following screen.

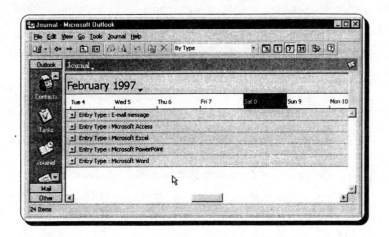

To find out how to use the various functions appearing on a Journal list, use the Help Assistant and search for 'journal'. On the displayed list, click the Journal radio button to obtain a similar help screen to that for Tasks. Try it, and also try the rest of the Help System. You will learn a lot.

* * *

Outlook has many more features, far too numerous to discuss in the space allocated in this book. What we have tried to do, is give you enough basic information so that you can have the confidence to explore the rest of Outlook's capabilities by yourself.

3. MICROSOFT WORD BASICS

Starting the Program

Word is started in Windows either by clicking the **Start** button then selecting **Program** and clicking on the 'Microsoft Word' icon on the cascade menu, clicking the Word icon on the Old Office Shortcut Bar, or by clicking the 'Open a Document' icon on the Office Shortcut Bar and double-clicking on a Word document file. In the latter case the document will be loaded into Word at the same time.

If you have used a previous version of Word it might be a good idea to use **The Office Assistant** and search for *what's new*. Selecting the 'What's New in Microsoft Word 97?' option (pointed to below), displays a further list of options which you might like to view.

What would you like to do?

- What's new in Microsoft Word 97?
- What's new with multilingual support?
- What's new with Web tools?
- What's new with reading online documents?
- What's new with WordMail?
- ▼ See more...

What's new

Search

Tips   Options   Close

The Word Screen:

The opening 'blank' screen of Word 97 is shown below. It is perhaps worth spending some time looking at the various parts that make up this screen. Word follows the usual Microsoft Windows conventions and if you are familiar with these you can skip through this section. Otherwise a few minutes might be well spent here.

The window as shown takes up the full screen area available. If you click on the application restore button, the top one of the two restore buttons at the top right of the screen, you can make Word show in a smaller window. This can be useful when you are running several applications at the same time and you want to transfer between them with the mouse.

Note that the Word window, which in this case displays an empty document with the title 'Document1', has a solid 'Title bar', indicating that it is the active application window. Although multiple windows can be displayed simultaneously, you can only enter data into the active window (which will always be displayed on top). Title bars of non active windows appear a lighter shade than that of the active one.

The Word screen is divided into several areas which have the following functions:

Area	*Function*
Command buttons	Clicking on the top command button, (see upper-left corner of the Word window), displays a pull-down menu which can be used to control the program window. It includes commands for restoring, moving, sizing, maximising, minimising, and closing the window. The lower command button controls the current document window in the same manner.
Title Bar	The bar at the top of a window which displays the application name and the name of the current document.
Minimise Button	When clicked on, this button minimises a document to an icon, or the application to the Windows Taskbar.
Restore Button	When clicked on, this button restores the active window to the position and size that was

occupied before it was maximised. The restore button is then replaced by a Maximise button, as shown here, which is used to set the window to full screen size.

Close button

The extreme top right button that you click to close a window.

Menu Bar

The bar below the Title bar which allows you to choose from several menu options. Clicking on a menu item displays the pull-down menu associated with that item.

Toolbar

The bar below the Menu bar which contains buttons that give you mouse click access to the functions most often used in the program. These are grouped according to function.

Formatting Bar

The buttons on the Formatting Bar allow you to change the attributes of a font, such as italic and underline, and also to format text in various ways. The Formatting Bar contains three boxes; a style box, a font box and a size box which show which style, font and size of characters are currently being used. These boxes give access to other installed styles, fonts and character sizes.

Ruler

The area where you can see and set tabulation points and indents.

Split Box	The area above the top vertical scroll button which when dragged allows you to split the screen.
Scroll Bars	The areas on the screen (extreme right and bottom of each window) that contain scroll boxes in vertical and horizontal bars. Clicking on these bars allows you to control the part of a document which is visible on the screen.
Scroll Arrows	The arrowheads at each end of each scroll bar at which you can click to scroll the screen up and down one line, or left and right 10% of the screen, at a time.
Selection Bar	The area on the screen in the left margin of the Word window (marked here with a box for convenience), where the mouse pointer changes to an arrow that slants to the right. Clicking the left mouse button once selects the current line, while clicking twice selects the current paragraph.
Insertion pointer	The pointer used to specify the place of text insertion.
Views Buttons	Clicking these buttons changes screen views quickly.
Status Bar	The bottom line of the document window that displays status information, and in which a short help description appears when you point and click on a button.

The Formatting Bar:

This is located below the Toolbar at the top of the Microsoft Word screen and is divided into seven sections, as shown below. They can only be accessed by clicking on them with the left mouse button.

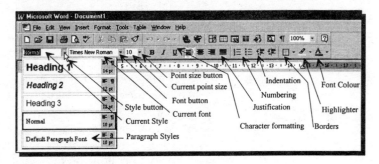

The Current Style box on the left of the Character formatting buttons, shows the style of the current paragraph; the one containing the cursor. By clicking the down-arrow button next to it, a list of all the available styles (with their font size) in the active template is produced, as shown. Clicking on one of these will change the style of the current paragraph.

To the right of the Style button is the Current font box which shows the current typeface. Clicking on the down-arrow button to the right of it allows you to change the typeface of any selected text. The Current point size box shows the size of selected characters which can be changed by clicking on the down-arrow button next to it and selecting another size from the displayed list.

Next, are three character formatting buttons which allow you to enhance selected text by emboldening, italicising, or underlining it. The next four buttons allow you to change the justification of a selected paragraph, and the next four help you set the different types of Numbering and Indentation options. The last three buttons allow you to add borders to selected text or objects, highlight or change font colour of selected text.

The Status Bar:

This is located at the bottom of the Word window and is used to display statistics about the active document.

For example, when a document is being opened, the Status bar displays for a short time its name and length in terms of total number of characters. Once a document is opened, the Status bar displays the statistics of the document at the insertion point; here it is on Page 1, Section 1, 11 characters from the left margin. Double-clicking the left of the status bar displays the Go To dialogue box, and double-clicking the other features will activate them. There is even help for WordPerfect users converting to Word. To activate this facility, double-click on **WPH**, or to make it 'permanent' use the **Help** command, select **WordPerfect Help,** click the **Options** button in the displayed dialogue box, and check the **Help for WordPerfect Users** box.

Note: If you do not need to have the **Help for WordPerfect Users** permanently available to you, it is a good idea not to set this option as it can have an adverse effect on the way you work. For example, if the WordPerfect Users help is switched on, you cannot delete sections of your document by highlighting them and pressing the <Del> key. We find this extremely annoying. Another annoying feature we found is that you will have to specify hanging indents separately for each paragraph without being able to carry the formatting from the first paragraph to the rest by simply pressing the <Enter> key. The list does not end with these two examples; there are many more!

Creating Word Documents

When the program is first used, all Word's features default to those shown on page 42. It is quite possible to use Word in this mode, without changing any main settings, but obviously it is possible to customise the package to your exact needs, as we shall see later.

Entering Text:

In order to illustrate some of Word's capabilities, you need to have a short text at hand. We suggest you type the memo displayed below into a new document. At this stage, don't worry if the length of the lines below differ from those on your display.

As you type in text, any time you want to force a new line, or paragraph, just press <Enter>. While typing within a paragraph, Word sorts out line lengths automatically (known as 'word wrap'), without you having to press any keys to move to a new line. If you make a mistake while typing, press the <BkSp> key enough times to erase the mistake and start again.

MEMO TO PC USERS
Networked Computers
The microcomputers in the Data Processing room are a mixture of IBM compatible PCs with either 486 or Pentium processors. They all have 3.5" floppy drives of 1.44MB capacity, and some also have CD-ROM drives. The PCs are connected to various printers via a network; the Laser printers available giving best output.

The computer you are using will have at least an 850MB capacity hard disc on which a number of software programs, including the latest version of Windows, have been installed. To make life easier, the hard disc is highly structured with each program installed in a separate folder (directory).

Moving Around a Document

You can move the cursor around a document with the normal direction keys, and with the key combinations listed below.

To move	*Press*
Left one character	←
Right one character	→
Up one line	↑
Down one line	↓
Left one word	Ctrl+←
Right one word	Ctrl+→
To beginning of line	Home
To end of line	End
To paragraph beginning	Ctrl+↑
To paragraph end	Ctrl+↓
Up one screen	PgUp
Down one screen	PgDn
To top of previous page	Ctrl+PgUp
To top of next page	Ctrl+PgDn
To beginning of file	Ctrl+Home
To end of file	Ctrl+End

In a multi-page document, use the **Edit**, **Go To** command (or <Ctrl+G>), shown here and to be explained shortly, to jump to a specified page number.

Obviously, you need to become familiar with the above methods of moving the cursor around a document, particularly if you are not using a mouse and you spot an error in a document which needs to be corrected, which is the subject of the latter half of this chapter.

Templates and Paragraph Styles

When you start Word for the first time, the Style Status box (at the extreme left of the Formatting bar) contains the word **Normal**. This means that all the text you have entered, at the moment, is shown in the Normal paragraph style which is one of the styles available in the NORMAL template. Every document produced by Word has to use a template, and NORMAL is the default. A template contains, both the document page settings and a set of formatting instructions which can be applied to text.

Changing Paragraph Styles:

To change the style of a paragraph, do the following:

- Place the cursor (insertion pointer) on the paragraph in question, say the title line

- Left click the Style Status button, and select the **Heading 1** style.

The selected paragraph reformats instantly in bold, and in Arial typeface of point size 14.

With the cursor in the second line of text, select **Heading 3** which reformats the line in Arial 12. Your memo should now look presentable, as shown below.

MEMO TO PC USERS

Networked Computers

The microcomputers in the Data Processing room are a mixture of IBM compatible PCs with either 486 or Pentium processors. They all have 3.5" floppy drives of 1.44MB capacity and some also have CD-ROM drives. The PCs are connected to various printers via a network; the Laser printers available giving best output.

The computer you are using will have at least an 850MB capacity hard disc on which a number of software programs, including the latest version of Windows, have been installed. To make life easier, the hard disc is highly structured with each program installed in a separate folder (directory).

Document Screen Displays

Word provides four display modes, Normal, Online, Page, Outline Layout, and Master Document, as well as the options to view your documents in a whole range of screen enlargements by selecting **Zoom**. You control all these viewing options with the **View** sub-menu, shown here, and when a document is displayed you can switch freely between them. When first loaded the screen displays in Normal mode.

The mode options have the following effect, and some can also be accessed by clicking the View buttons on the left of the Status bar.

Normal

Returns you to normal viewing from either Online, Page or Outline Layout, or Master Document viewing mode.

Online Layout

A view that optimises the layout of a document to make online reading easier. For example, text appears larger and wraps to fit the window, rather than the way it would actually print.

In online layout view, Word automatically displays the Document Map, a separate pane that you can use to navigate around your document or track your location in it.

Page Layout

Provides a WYSIWYG (what you see is what you get) view of a document. The text displays in the typefaces and point sizes you specify, and with the selected attributes (alignment, indention, spacing, etc.). All text boxes or frames, tables, graphics, headers, footers, and footnotes appear on the screen as they will in the final printed document.

Outline

Provides a collapsible view of a document, which enables you to see its organisation at a glance. You can display all the text in a file, or just the text that uses the paragraph styles you specify. Using this mode, allows you to quickly rearrange large sections of text.

Some people like to create an outline of their document first, consisting of all the headings, then to sort out the document structure and finally fill in the text.

Master Document

Provides you with an outline view of a document that takes its contents from one or more Word documents. For example, each chapter of a book could be made into a sub-document of such a Master Document.

The Master Document could then be used to reorganise, add or remove sub-documents. Selecting this mode, causes Word to display the Master Document and Outline toolbars.

Full Screen

Presents you with a clean, uncluttered screen; the Toolbars, Ruler, Scroll bars, and Status bar are removed. To return to the usual screen, click the 'Full Screen' icon, shown here, which appears at the bottom of your screen when in this mode.

Zoom

Allows you to change the viewing magnification factor from its default value of 100%. This can also be changed by clicking the 'Zoom Control' icon on the Toolbar. Clicking its down arrow button, reveals other magnification factors, as shown here.

Changing Default Options

Modifying Margins:

To change the standard page margins for your entire document from the cursor position onward, or for selected text (more about this later), do the following:

- Select the **File, Page Setup** command
- Click the left mouse button at the **Margins** tab on the displayed dialogue box, shown below.

The 'Preview' page to the right of the box shows how your changes will look on a real page.

Changing the Default Paper Size:

To change the default paper size from the size set during installation to a different size, do the following:

- Select the **File, Page Setup** command
- Click the left mouse button at the **Paper Size** tab on the displayed dialogue box

- Click the down-arrow against the **Paper Size** box to reveal the list of available paper sizes

- Change the page size to your new choice, and press the **Default** button and confirm that you wish this change to affect all new documents based on the Normal template.

Check that the paper size matches that in your printer, otherwise you may get strange results. The orientation of the printed page is normally **Portrait** (text prints across the page width), but you could choose to change this to **Landscape** which prints across the page length, as long as your printer can print in landscape.

All changes you can make to your document from the Page Setup dialogue box can be applied to either the whole document or to the rest of the document starting from the current position of the insertion pointer. To carry out such changes click the down-arrow button against the **Apply to** box and choose appropriately from the drop-down menu list.

Modifying the Paper Source:

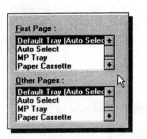

Clicking on the third Page Setup tab, displays yet another dialogue box, part of which is shown here, from which you can select the paper source. You might have a printer that holds paper in trays, in which case you might want to specify that the first page (headed paper perhaps), should be taken from one tray, while the rest of the paper should be taken from a different tray.

Modifying the Page Layout:

Clicking the last Page Setup tab displays the Layout dialogue box, part of which is shown here. From this dialogue box you can set options for headers and footers, section breaks, vertical alignment and whether to add line numbers.

The default for **Section Start** is 'New Page' which allows the section to start at the top of the next page. Pressing the down arrow against this option, allows you to change this choice.

In the Headers and Footers box you can specify whether you want one header or footer for even-numbered pages and a different header or footer for odd-numbered pages. You can further specify if you want a different header or footer on the first page from the header or footer used for the rest of the document. Word can align the top line with the 'Top' margin, but this can be changed with the **Vertical Alignment** option.

Changing Other Default Options:

You can also change the default options available to you in Word 97, by selecting the **Tools, Options** command. Using the displayed Options dialogue box below, you can, amongst other things, do the following:

* Specify the default **View** options. For example, you can select whether non-printing characters, such as Tabs, Spaces, and Paragraph marks, are shown or not.

* Adjust the **General** Word settings, such as background repagination, display of the recently used file-list, and selection of units of measure.

* Adjust the **Print** settings, such as allowing background printing, reverse print order, or choose to print comments with documents.

* Change the **Save** options, such as selecting to always create a backup copy of your work.

Saving to a File

To save a document to disc, use either of the following two commands:

- **File, Save** (or click the Save toolbar icon) which is used when a document has previously been saved to disc in a named file; using this command automatically saves your work under the existing filename without prompting you.

- **File, Save As** command which is used when you want to save your document with a different name from the one you gave it already.

Using the **File, Save As** command (or the very first time you use the **File, Save** command when a document has no name), causes the following dialogue box to appear on your screen:

Note that the first 255 characters of the first paragraph in your document is highlighted in the **File name** field box and the program is waiting for you to type a new name. Any name you type (less than 255 characters) will replace the existing name. Filenames cannot include any of the following keyboard characters: /, \, >, <, *, ?, ", |, :, or ;. Word adds the file extension **.doc** automatically and uses it to identify its documents.

You can select a drive other than the one displayed, by clicking the down arrow against the **Save in** field. You can also select a folder in which to save your work. If you do not have a suitably named folder, then you can create one using the Create New Folder button on the Save As dialogue box, shown below.

We used this facility to create a folder called **Docs** within the **My Documents** folder in the C: drive.

To save our work currently in memory, we selected the **Docs** folder in the **Save in** field of the Save As dialogue box, then moved the cursor into the **File name** box, and typed **Pcusers 1**. We suggest you do the same.

By clicking the **Save as type** button at the bottom of the Save As dialogue box, you can save the Document Template, or the Text Only parts of your work, or you can save your document in a variety of other formats, including rich text, WordPerfect, and HTML.

59

Selecting File Location:

You can select where Word is to look automatically for your document files when you first choose to open or save a document by selecting the **Tools, Options** command, click the File Locations tab of the displayed Options dialogue box, and modifying the location of the document files, as shown below.

As you can see, the default location of other types of files is also given in the above dialogue box.

Microsoft suggests that you store documents, worksheets, presentations, databases, and other files you are currently working on, in the **My Documents** folder. This, of course, is a matter of preference, so we leave it to you to decide.

Document Properties:

A useful feature in Word is the facility to add document properties to every file by selecting the **File, Properties** command. A Properties box, as shown below, opens for you to type additional information about your document.

In this box you can select to add a manager, company, or category name to group files together for ease of retrieval.

To do this on a more regular basis, make sure that the **Prompt for Document Properties** box in the Save Options dialogue box (use the **Tools, Options** command and click the Save tab of the Options dialogue box) is selected and appears ticked.

Closing a Document:

There are several ways to close a document in Word. Once you have saved it you can click its 'X' close button, or double-click on the Document Control button at the left end of the menu bar; you would usually use these when you have several files open together.

If you want to close the current document, and then open a new one or a different one, do the following:

- Choose **File, Close** to close the current document (remove it from your computer's memory) before using either

- **File, New** (or clicking) to create a new file, or

- **File, Open** (or clicking) to use an existing file.

If the document (or file) has changed since the last time it was saved, you will be given the option to save it before it is removed from memory.

If a document is not closed before a new document is opened, then both documents will be held in memory, but only one will be the current document. To find out which documents are held in memory, use the **Window** command to reveal the following menu:

In this case, the first document in the list is the current document, and to make another document the current one, either type the document number, or point at its name and click the left mouse button.

To close a document which is not the current document, use the **Window** command, make it current, and close it with one of the above methods.

4. EDITING WORD DOCUMENTS

It will not be long, when using Word, before you will need to edit your document. One of the first things you will notice is that misspelled words are unobtrusively underlined in a red wavy line, as shown here, and that ungrammatical phrases are similarly underlined in green. Right-clicking these words or phrases allows you to correct them. This is possibly the most time-saving enhancement in the spell and grammar checker (to be discussed later).

Other editing could include deleting unwanted words or adding extra text in the document. All these operations are very easy to carry out. For small deletions, such as letters or words, the easiest method to adopt is the use of the <Del> or <BkSp> keys. With the <Del> key, position the cursor on the left of the first letter you want to delete and press <Del>; the letter is deleted and the following text moves one space to the left. With the <BkSp> key, position the cursor immediately to the right of the character to be deleted and press <BkSp>; the cursor moves one space to the left pulling the rest of the line with it and overwriting the character to be deleted.

Word processing is usually carried out in the insert mode. Any characters typed will be inserted at the cursor location (insertion point) and the following text will be pushed to the right, and down, to make room. To insert blank lines in your text, place the cursor at the beginning of the line where the blank line is needed and press <Enter>. To remove the blank line, position the cursor on it and press <Del>.

When larger scale editing is needed you have several alternatives. You could first 'select' the text to be altered, then use the **Cut, Copy** and **Paste** operations available in the **Edit** sub-menu, or click on Toolbar button alternatives. Another method is to use the 'drag and drop' facility for copying or moving text.

Selecting Text

The procedure in Word, as with most Windows based applications, is first to select the text to be altered before any operation, such as formatting or editing, can be carried out on it. Selected text is highlighted on the screen. This can be carried out in two main ways:

A. Using the keyboard, to select:

- A block of text.

  Position the cursor on the first character to be selected and hold down the <Shift> key while using the arrow keys to highlight the required text, then release the <Shift> key.

- A word.

  Use <Shift+End>.

- From the present cursor position to the beginning of the line.

  Use <Shift+Home>.

- From the present cursor position to the end of the document.

  Use <Shift+Ctrl+End>.

- From the present cursor position to the beginning of the document.

  Use <Shift+Ctrl+Home>.

B. *With the mouse, to select:*

- A block of text.

  Press down the left mouse button at the beginning of the block and while holding it pressed, drag the cursor across the block so that the desired text is highlighted, then release the mouse button.

- A word.

  Double-click within the word.

- A line.

  Place the mouse pointer on the selection bar, just to the left of the line, and click once (for multiple lines, after selecting the first line, drag the pointer in the selection bar).

- A sentence.

  Hold the <Ctrl> key down and click in the sentence.

- A paragraph.

  Place the mouse pointer in the selection bar and double-click (for multiple paragraphs, after selecting the first paragraph, drag the pointer in the selection bar).

- The whole document.

  Place the mouse pointer in the selection bar, hold the <Ctrl> key down and click once.

Copying Blocks of Text

Once text has been selected it can be copied to another location in your present document, to another Word document, or to another Windows application, via the clipboard. As with most of the editing and formatting operations there are several alternative ways of doing this, as follows:

- Use the **Edit, Copy** command sequence from the menu, to copy the selected text to the Windows clipboard, moving the cursor to the start of where you want the copied text to be placed, and using the **Edit, Paste** command.

- Use the quick key combinations, <Ctrl+Ins> (or <Ctrl+C>) to copy and <Shift+Ins> (or <Ctrl+V>) to paste, once the text to be copied has been selected, which does not require the menu bar to be activated.

- Use the 'Copy to clipboard' and 'Paste from clipboard' Toolbar buttons; you can of course only use this method with a mouse.

  To copy the same text again to another location, or to any open document window or application, move the cursor to the new location and paste it there with any of these methods. It is stored on the clipboard until it is replaced by the next Cut, or Copy operation.

- First select the text, then hold both the <Ctrl> and <Shift> keys depressed, place the cursor at the start of where you want the copied text to be and press the right mouse button. The new text will insert itself where placed, even if the overstrike mode is in operation. Text copied by this method is not placed on the clipboard, so multiple copies are not possible, as with the other methods.

Moving Blocks of Text

Selected text can be moved to any location in the same document by either of the following:

- Using the **Edit, Cut,** command or <Shift+Del> (or <Ctrl+X>).

- Clicking the 'Cut to clipboard' Toolbar button, shown here.

Next, move the cursor to the required new location and use either of the following procedures:

- The **Edit, Paste** command.

- Any other paste actions as described previously.

The moved text will be placed at the cursor location and will force any existing text to make room for it. This operation can be cancelled by simply pressing <Esc>. Once moved, multiple copies of the same text can be produced by other **Paste** operations.

Selected text can be moved by dragging the mouse with the left button held down. The drag pointer is an arrow with an attached square - the vertical dotted line showing the point of insertion.

Deleting Blocks of Text

When text is 'cut' it is removed from the document, but placed on the clipboard until further text is either copied or cut. With Word any selected text can be deleted by pressing **Edit, Cut,** or by pressing the <Del>, or <BkSp> keys. However, using **Edit, Cut,** allows you to use the **Edit, Paste** command, but using the <Del> or <BkSp> keys, does not.

The Undo Command

As text is lost with the delete command, you should use it with caution, but if you do make a mistake all is not lost as long as you act promptly. The **Edit, Undo** command or <Ctrl+Z> (or <Alt+BkSp>) reverses your most recent editing or formatting commands.

You can also use the Toolbar buttons, shown here,
 to undo one of several editing or formatting mistakes (press the down arrow to the right of the left button to see a list of your changes) or even redo any one of the undo moves with the right button.

Undo does not reverse any action once editing changes have been saved to file. Only editing done since the last save can be reversed.

Finding and Changing Text

Word allows you to search for specifically selected text, or character combinations. To do this use the **Find** or the **Replace** option from the **Edit** command sub-menu.

Using the **Find** option (<Ctrl+F>), will highlight each occurrence of the supplied text in turn so that you can carry out some action on it, such as change its font or appearance.

Using the **Replace** option (<Ctrl+H>), allows you to specify what replacement is to be automatically carried out. For example, in a long article you may decide to replace every occurrence of the word 'microcomputers' with the word 'PCs'.

To illustrate the **Replace** procedure, either select the option from the **Edit** sub-menu or use the quick key combination <Ctrl+H>. This opens the Find and Replace dialogue box shown on the next page.

Clicking the **More** button displays the top half of the composite screen dump shown below.

Towards the bottom of the dialogue box, there are five check boxes; the first two can be used to match the case of letters in the search string, and/or a whole word, while the last three can be used for wildcard, 'sounds like' or 'word forms' matching.

The two buttons, **Format** and **Special**, situated at the bottom of the dialogue box, let you control how the search is carried out. The lists of available options, when either of these buttons is pressed, are displayed above. You will of course only see one or the other, but not both as shown here.

You can force both the search and the replace operations to work with exact text attributes. For example, selecting:

- The **Font** option from the list under **Format**, displays a dialogue box in which you select a font (such as Arial, Times New Roman, etc.); a font-style (such as regular, bold, italic, etc.); an underline option (such as single, double, etc.); and special effects (such as strike-through, superscript, subscript, etc.).

- The **Paragraph** option, lets you control indentation, spacing (before and after), and alignment.

- The **Style** option, allows you to search for, or replace, different paragraph styles. This can be useful if you develop a new style and want to change all the text of another style in a document to use your preferred style.

With the use of the **Special** button, you can search for, and replace, various specified document marks, tabs, hard returns, etc., or a combination of both these and text, as listed in the previous screen dump.

Below we list only two of the many key combinations of special characters that could be typed into the **Find what** and **Replace with** boxes when the **Use wildcards** box is checked.

Type	*To find or replace*
?	Any single character within a pattern. For example, searching for nec?, will find <u>neck</u>, con<u>nect</u>, etc.
*	Any string of characters. For example, searching for c*r, will find such words as <u>cellar</u>, <u>chillier</u>, etc., also parts of words such as <u>character</u>, and combinations of words such as <u>connect, cellar</u>

Page Breaks

The program automatically inserts a 'soft' page break in a document when a page of typed text is full. To force a manual, or hard page break, either type <Ctrl+Enter> or use the **Insert**, **Break** command and select **Page Break** in the dialogue box, as shown below.

Pressing **OK** places a series of dots across the page to indicate the page break, as shown below. To delete manual page breaks place the cursor on the selection bar to the left of the page break mark, click once to highlight the line of dots, and press <Del>.

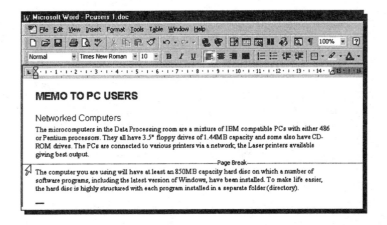

Soft page breaks which are automatically entered by the program at the end of pages, cannot be deleted.

Using the Spell Checker

The package has a very comprehensive spell checker which whenever it thinks it has found a misspelled word, underlines it with a red wavy line. To correct your document, right-click such words for alternatives.

However, the spell checker can also be used in another way. To spell check your document, either click the 'Spelling' button on the Standard Toolbar, shown here, or use the **Tools**, **Spelling and Grammar** command (or **F7**) to open the dialogue box shown below (if necessary, use the **Tools, Language** command, select the correct dictionary and click the **Default** button).

Word starts spell checking from the point of insertion onwards. If you want to spell check the whole document, move the insertion pointer to the beginning of the document before starting. If you want to check a word or paragraph only, highlight it first. Once Word has found a misspelled word, you can either correct it in the Not in Dictionary box, or select a word from the **Suggestions** list.

The main dictionary cannot be edited. However, the system has the ability to add specialised and personal dictionaries with the facility to customise and edit them. If you are using a personal dictionary and choose **Add**, the specified word is added to that dictionary.

72

Printing Documents

When Windows was first installed on your computer the printers you intend to use should have been selected, and the SETUP program should have installed the appropriate printer drivers. Before printing for the first time, you would be wise to ensure that your printer is in fact properly installed. To do this, click on **Start** then select **S**ettings and click the **P**rinters menu option to open the Printers dialogue box shown below.

Here, two printer drivers have been installed; an HP LaserJet 5MP as the 'default' printer and an HP LaserJet 5/5M PostScript. In our case these are both configured to output to a printer via the parallel port LPT1. This refers to the socket at the back of your PC which is connected to your printer. LPT1 is short for Line Printer No. 1. Your selections may, obviously, not be the same.

To see how a printer is configured (whether to print to the parallel port or to a file), select it by clicking its icon, use the **F**ile, **P**roperties command and click the Details tab of the displayed dialogue box.

Opening a Word Document:

Next, return to or reactivate Word and, if the document

you want to print is not in memory, either click the 'Open' button on the Toolbar, or use the **F**ile, **O**pen command, to display the Open dialogue box shown overleaf.

Use this dialogue box to locate the file (document) you want to print, which will be found on the drive and folder (directory) on which you saved it originally. Select it and click the **Open** button (or double-click its name), to load it into your computer's memory.

To print your document, do one of the following:

- Click the Print icon on the Toolbar, shown here, which prints the document using the current defaults.

- Use the **File, Print** command which opens the 'Print' box, shown below.

The settings in the Print dialogue box allow you to select the number of copies, and which pages, you want printed. You can also select to print the document, the summary information relating to that document, comments, styles, etc., as shown in the drop-down list also on the previous page.

You can even change the selected printer by clicking the down arrow against the **Printer Name** box which displays the available printers on your system.

Clicking the **Properties** button on the Print dialogue box, displays the Properties dialogue box for the selected printer, shown below, which allows you to select the paper size, orientation needed, paper source, etc.

The **Options** button on the Print dialogue box, gives you access to some more advanced print options, such as printing in reverse order, with or without comments (annotations), print hidden text or field codes, etc.

Clicking the **OK** button on these various multi-level dialogue boxes, causes Word to accept your selections and return you to the previous level dialogue box, until the Print dialogue box is reached. Selecting **OK** on this first level dialogue box, sends print output from Word to your selection, either the printer connected to your computer, or to an encoded file on disc. Selecting **Cancel** or **Close** on any level dialogue box, aborts the selections made at that level.

Do remember that, whenever you change printers, the appearance of your document may change, as Word uses the fonts available with the newly selected printer. This can affect the line lengths, which in turn will affect both the tabulation and pagination of your document.

Before printing to paper, click the Print Preview icon on the Toolbar, shown here, or use the **File, Print Preview** command, to see how much of your document will fit on your selected page size. This depends very much on the chosen font. Thus, the **Print Preview** option allows you to see the layout of the final printed page, which can save a few trees and equally important to you, a lot of frustration and wear and tear on your printer. To return to your working document from a print preview display, click the **Close** button on the Print Preview menu bar.

Other enhancements of your document, such as selection of fonts, formatting of text, and pagination, will be discussed in the next chapter.

5. FORMATTING WORD DOCUMENTS

Formatting involves the appearance of individual words or even characters, the line spacing and alignment of paragraphs, and the overall page layout of the entire document. These functions are carried out in Word in several different ways.

Primary page layout is included in a document's Template and text formatting in a Template's styles. Within any document, however, you can override Paragraph Style formats by applying text formatting and enhancements manually to selected text. To immediately cancel manual formatting, select the text and use the

Edit, Undo

command, or (<Ctrl+Z>). The selected text reverts to its original format.

In the long term, you can cancel manual formatting by selecting the text and using the <Shift+Ctrl+N> key stroke. The text then reverts to its style format.

Formatting Text

If you use TrueType fonts, which are automatically installed when you set up Windows, Word uses the same font to display text on the screen and to print on paper. The screen fonts provide a very close approximation of printed characters. TrueType font names are preceded by ᴛᴛ in the Font box on the Formatting toolbar and in the Font dialogue box which displays when you use the **Format, Font** command.

If you use non-TrueType fonts, then use a screen font that matches your printer font. If a matching font is not available, or if your printer driver does not provide screen font information, Windows chooses the screen font that most closely resembles the printer font.

Originally, the title and subtitle of the **Pcusers 1** memo, were typed in the 14 and 12 point size Arial typeface, respectively, while the main text was typed in 10 point size Times New Roman.

To change this memo into what appears on the screen dump displayed below, first select the title of the memo and format it to bold, italics, 18 point size Arial and centre it between the margins, then select the subtitle and format it to bold, 14 point size Arial.

Finally select each paragraph of the main body of the memo in turn, and format it to 12 point size Times New Roman. All of this formatting can be achieved by using the buttons on the Formatting bar shown below (see also the section entitled 'Paragraph Alignment').

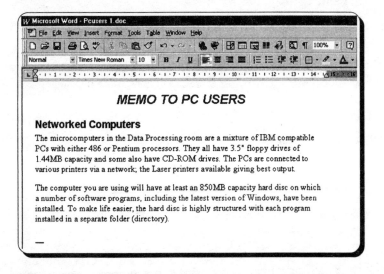

If you can't access these font styles, it will probably be because your printer does not support them, in which case you will need to select other fonts that are supported.

Save the result under the new filename **Pcusers 2**, using the **File, Save As** command.

In Word all manual formatting, including the selection of font, point size, style (bold, italic, highlight, strike-through, hidden and capitals), colour, super/subscript, and various underlines, are carried out by first selecting the text and then executing the formatting command.

The easiest way of activating the formatting commands is from the Formatting toolbar. Another way is to use the **Format, Font** command, which displays the following dialogue box:

Yet another method is by using quick keys, some of which are listed below:

To Format	Type
Bold	Ctrl+B
Italic	Ctrl+I
Underline	Ctrl+U
Word underline	Ctrl+Shift+W
Double underline	Ctrl+Shift+D

There are quick keys to do almost anything, but the problem is remembering them! The ones listed here are the most useful and the easiest to remember.

Text Enhancements

Word defines a paragraph, as any text which is followed by a paragraph mark, which is created by pressing the <Enter> key. So single line titles, as well as long typed text, can form paragraphs.

 The paragraph symbol, shown here, is only visible in your text if you have selected it from the Toolbar.

Paragraph Alignment:

Word allows you to align a paragraph at the left margin (the default), at the right margin, centred between both margins, or justified between both margins. As with most operations there are several ways to perform alignment in Word. Three such methods are:

- Using buttons on the **Formatting bar**.
- Using keyboard short cuts, when available.
- Using the **Format**, **Paragraph** menu command.

The table below describes the buttons on the Formatting bar and their keystroke shortcuts.

Buttons on Formatting bar	Paragraph Alignment	Keystrokes
	Left	<Ctrl+L>
	Centred	<Ctrl+E>
	Right	<Ctrl+R>
	Justified	<Ctrl+J>

The display below shows the dialogue box resulting from using the **Format**, **Paragraph** command in which you can specify any **Left, Right**, or **Special** indentation required.

Paragraph Spacing:

The above Paragraph dialogue box can also be used to display a paragraph on screen, or print it on paper, in single-line, 1½-line, or double-line spacing. You can even set the spacing to any value you want by using the **At Least** option, as shown on the above screen dump, then specify what interval you want.

The available shortcut keys for paragraph spacing are as follows:

To Format	Type
Single-spaced lines	Ctrl+1
One-and-a-half-spaced lines	Ctrl+5
Double-spaced lines	Ctrl+2

Whichever of the above methods is used, formatting can take place either before or after the text is entered. If formatting is selected first, then text will type in the chosen format until a further formatting command is given. If, on the other hand, you choose to enter text and then format it afterwards, you must first select the text to be formatted, then activate the formatting.

Word gives you the choice of 4 units to work with, inches, centimetres, points or picas. These can be selected by using the **Tools**, **Options** command, choosing the **General** tab of the displayed Options dialogue box, and clicking the down arrow against the **Measurement units** list box, shown open here, which is to be found at the bottom of the dialogue box.

Indenting Text:

Most documents will require some form of paragraph indenting. An indent is the space between the margin and the edge of the text in the paragraph. When an indent is set (on the left or right side of the page), any justification on that side of the page sets at the indent, not the page border.

To illustrate indentation, open the file **Pcusers 2**, select the first paragraph, and then choose the **Format**, **Paragraph** command. In the **Indentation** field, select 2.5cm for both **Left** and **Right**, as shown on the next page. On clicking **OK**, the first selected paragraph is displayed indented. Our screen dump shows the result of the indentation as well as the settings on the Paragraph dialogue box which caused it.

The **Indentation** option in the Paragraph dialogue box, can be used to create 'hanging' indents, where all the lines in a paragraph, including any text on the first line that follows a tab, are indented by a specified amount. This is often used in lists to emphasise certain points.

To illustrate the method, use the **Pcusers 1** file and add at the end of it the text shown below. After you have typed the text in, save the enlarged memo as **Pcusers 3**, before going on with formatting the new information.

In Windows you can work with files in three different ways:

Name Description

My Computer Use the My Computer utility which Microsoft have spent much time and effort making as intuitive as possible.

Explorer Use the Windows Explorer, a much-improved version of the older File Manager.

MS-DOS Use an MS-DOS Prompt window if you prefer to and are an expert with the DOS commands.

Saving the work at this stage is done as a precaution in case anything goes wrong with the formatting - it is sometimes much easier to reload a saved file (using the **File**, **Open** command), than it is to try to unscramble a wrongly formatted document!

Next, highlight the last 4 paragraphs above, use the **Format**, **Paragraph** command, and select 'Hanging' under **Special** and 3 cm under **By**. On clicking the **OK** button, the text formats as shown, but it is still highlighted. To remove the highlighting, click the mouse button anywhere on the page. The second and following lines of the paragraphs selected, should be indented 3 cm from the left margin, as shown below.

This is still not very inspiring, so to complete the effect we will edit the first lines of each paragraph as follows:

Place the cursor in front of the word 'Description' and press the <Tab> key once. This places the start of the word in the same column as the indented text of the other paragraphs. To complete the effect place tabs before the words 'Use' in the next three paragraphs, until your hanging indents are correct, as shown on the next page.

In Windows you can work with files in three different ways:

Name	Description
My Computer	Use the My Computer utility which Microsoft have spent much time and effort making as intuitive as possible.
Explorer	Use the Windows Explorer, a much-improved version of the older File Manager.
MS-DOS	Use an MS-DOS Prompt window if you prefer to and are an expert with the DOS commands.

This may seem like a complicated rigmarole to go through each time you want the hanging indent effect, but with Word you will eventually set up all your indents, etc., as styles in templates. Then all you do is click in a paragraph to produce them.

 When you finish formatting the document, save it under its current filename either with the **File**, **Save** command (<Ctrl+S>), or by clicking the Save button. This command does not display a dialogue box, so you use it when you do not need to make any changes to the saving operation.

Inserting Bullets:

Bullets are small characters you can insert, anywhere you like, in the text of your document to improve visual impact. In Word there are several choices for displaying lists with bullets or numbers. As well as the two Formatting bar buttons, others are made available through the **Format, Bullets and Numbering** command, which displays the following dialogue box.

You can select any of the bullets shown here, and then you could click the **Customize** button to change the shape and size of the bullet, or the indentation.

Further, by pressing the **Bullet** button on the Customized Bulleted List dialogue box which would be displayed, you could select any character from the Symbol typeface or other available type-faces.

If you select the **Numbered** or **Outline Numbered** tab, a similar dialogue box is displayed, giving you a choice of several numbering or outline (multilevel) systems.

Once inserted, you can copy, move or cut a bulleted line in the same way as any other text. However, you can not delete a bullet with the <BkSp> or <Del> keys.

Formatting with Page Tabs

You can format text in columns by using tab stops. Word has default left tab stops every 1.27 cm from the left margin, as shown here. This symbol appears on the left edge of the ruler (see below).

To set tabs, use either the **Format**, **Tabs** command which produces the Tab dialogue box, or click on the tab symbol on the left of the Ruler which cycles through the available tab stops.

The tab stop types available have the following function:

Button	*Name*	*Effect*
	Left	Left aligns text after the tab stop.
	Centre	Centres text on tab stop.
	Right	Right aligns text after the tab stop.
	Decimal	Aligns decimal point with tab stop.

87

To clear the ruler of tab settings press the **Clear All** button in the Tabs dialogue box. When you set a tab stop on the ruler, all default tab stops to the left of the one you are setting are removed. In addition, tab stops apply either to the paragraph containing the cursor, or to any selected paragraphs.

The easiest way to set a tab is to click on the tab type button you want and then point and click at the required position on the lower half of the ruler. To remove an added tab, point to it, click and drag it off the ruler.

If you want tabular text to be separated by characters instead of by spaces, select one of the three available characters from the **Leader** box in the Tabs dialogue box. The options are none (the default), dotted, dashed, or underline. The Contents and Index pages of this book are set with right tabs and dotted leader characters.

Note: As all paragraph formatting, such as tab stops, is placed at the end of a paragraph, if you want to carry the formatting of the current paragraph to the next, press <Enter>. If you don't want formatting to carry on, press the down arrow key instead.

Formatting with Styles

We saw earlier on page 50, how you can format your work using Paragraph Styles, but we confined ourselves to using the default **Normal** style only. In this section we will get to grips with how to create, modify, use, and manage styles.

As mentioned previously, a Paragraph Style is a set of formatting instructions which you save so that you can use it repeatedly within a document or in different documents. A collection of Paragraph Styles can be placed in a Template which could be appropriate for, say, all your memos, so it can be used to preserve uniformity. It maintains consistency and saves time by not having to format each paragraph individually.

Further, should you decide to change a style, all the paragraphs associated with that style reformat automatically. Finally, if you want to provide a pattern for shaping a final document, then you use what is known as a Template. All documents which have not been assigned a document template, use the **Normal.dot** global template, by default.

Paragraph Styles:

Paragraph Styles contain paragraph and character formats and a name can be attached to these formatting instructions. From then on, applying the style name is the same as formatting that paragraph with the same instructions.

You can create a style by example, using either the Formatting bar or the keyboard, or you can create a style from scratch, before you use it, by selecting the **Format, Style** menu command. By far the simplest way of creating a style is by example.

Creating Paragraph Styles by Example: Previously, we spent some time manually creating some hanging indents in the last few paragraphs of the **Pcusers 3** document. To create a style from this previous work, place the insertion pointer in one of these paragraphs, say, in the 'Name Description' line, and highlight the entire name of the existing style in the Formatting bar's Style box, as shown below.

In Windows you can work with files in three different ways:

Name	Description
My Computer	Use the My Computer utility which Microsoft have spent much time and effort making as intuitive as possible.
Explorer	Use the Windows Explorer, a much-improved version of the older File Manager.

Then, type the new style name you want to create, say, 'Hanging Indent', and press <Enter>.

Finally, highlight the last three paragraphs with hanging indents and change their style to the new 'Hanging Indent', by clicking the mouse in the Style box button and selecting the appropriate style from the displayed list, as shown below. Save the result as **Pcusers 4.**

Creating Styles with the Menu Command: You can create, or change, a style before you apply any formatting to a paragraph, by using the **Format**, **Style** command. This displays the Style dialogue box, in which you can choose which style you want to change from the displayed **Styles** list.

Having selected the style you want to change (or not, as the case may be), click the **Modify** button which produces the Modify Style dialogue box. From here you can create a new style, or modify an existing style, by changing the formatting of characters, borders, paragraphs, and tab stops. You can even select which style should follow your current style.

Finally, have a look at Word's built-in styles by selecting **Style Gallery** from the **Format** menu.

Document Templates

A document template provides the overall pattern of your final document. It can contain:

- Styles to control your paragraph and formats.

- Page set-up options.

- Boilerplate text, which is text that remains the same in every document.

- AutoText, which is standard text and graphics that you could insert in a document by typing the name of the AutoText entry.

- Macros, which are programs that can change the menus and key assignments to comply with the type of document you are creating.

- Customised shortcuts, toolbars and menus.

If you don't assign a template to a document, then the default **Normal.dot** template is used by Word. To create a new document template, you either modify an existing one, create one from scratch, or create one based on the formatting of an existing document.

Creating a Document Template:

To illustrate the last point above, we will create a simple document template, which we will call **Pcuser**, based on the formatting of the **Pcusers 4** document. But first, make sure you have defined the 'Hanging Indent' style as explained earlier.

To create a template based on an existing document do the following:

- Open the existing document.

- Select the **File, Save As** command which displays the Save As dialogue box, shown overleaf.

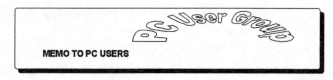

- In the **Save as type** box, select Document Template.

- In the **Save in** box, use the Templates folder which is in the Msoffice folder, which should have opened for you.

- In the **File name** box, type the name of the new template (PCuser in our example).

- Press the **Save** button, which opens the template file **Pcuser.dot** in the Word working area.

- Add the text and graphics you want to appear in all new documents that you base on this template, and *delete* any items (including text) you do not want to appear. In our example, we deleted everything in the document, bar the heading, and added the words 'PC User Group' using **Insert, Picture, WordArt**, to obtain:

- Click the Save icon on the Toolbar, and close the document.

To use the new template, do the following:

- Use the **File**, **New** command which causes the New dialogue box to be displayed, as shown below.

- Click the General tab and select the name of the template you want to use from the displayed list.
- Make sure that the radio button **Document** is selected, and click the **OK** button.

The new document will be using the selected template.

Templates can also contain Macros as well as AutoText; macros allow you to automate Word keystroke actions only, while AutoText speeds up the addition of boilerplate text and graphics into your document. However, the design of these features is beyond the scope of this book.

On the other hand, Word has a series of built-in templates to suit every occasion. These can be found, as seen in the above dialogue box, under the tabs of Letters & Faxes, Memos, Reports, etc. Try them.

* * *

Word has many more features, far too numerous to mention in the space allocated to this book, although we will be discussing later on how you can use Word to share information with other MS applications and how to use mail merge techniques. What we have tried to do so far, is give you enough basic information so that you can have the confidence to forge ahead and explore the rest of Word's capabilities by yourself.

Perhaps, you might consider exploring page numbering, headers and footers, tables, frames, drawing, and outlining, in that order. We leave it to you. However, if you would prefer to be guided through these topics, then may we suggest you look up the later chapters of the book *MS Word 97 explained* (BP428), also published by BERNARD BABANI (publishing) Ltd.

* * *

6. THE EXCEL SPREADSHEET

Microsoft Excel is a powerful and versatile software package which, over the last few years, has proved its usefulness, not only in the business world, but with scientific and engineering users as well.

The program's power lies in its ability to emulate everything that can be done by the use of pencil, paper and a calculator. Thus, it is an 'electronic spreadsheet' or simply a 'spreadsheet', a name which is also used to describe it and other similar products. Its power is derived from the power of the computer it is running on, and the flexibility and accuracy with which it can deal with the solution of the various applications it is programmed to manage. These can vary from budgeting and forecasting to the solution of complex scientific and engineering problems.

Starting the Excel Program

Excel is started in Windows 95 either by clicking the **Start** button then selecting **Program** and clicking on the 'Microsoft Excel' icon on the cascade menu, or by clicking the Excel icon on the Old Office Shortcut Bar, or by clicking the 'Open a Document' icon on the Office Shortcut Bar and double-clicking on an Excel worksheet file. In the latter case the worksheet will be loaded into Excel at the same time.

The first time you use Excel, it might be a good idea to activate the Assistant and type 'what's new', in the text box, then click **Search**.

This causes the following Help screen to be displayed.

Clicking the What's new in Microsoft Excel 97 menu option, opens up the Key information for upgraders and new users help screen, from which you can find out differences between this version of Excel and previous versions of the program.

We suggest you spend a little time here browsing through the various help screens. After doing so, click the **Help Topics** button at the top left of the dialogue box to obtain further information on Excel 97. Below, we show all the help books open so that you can see the wealth of information contained in them.

The Excel Screen

When Excel is loaded, a 'blank' spreadsheet screen displays with a similar Title bar, Menu bar, Toolbar and Formatting bar to those of Word. Obviously there are some differences, but that is to be expected as the two programs serve different purposes.

The opening screen of Excel is shown below. It is perhaps worth looking at the various parts that make up this screen, or window, if only to see how similar it is to that of Word. Excel follows the usual Microsoft Windows conventions with which you should be very familiar by now.

The window as shown above takes up the full screen area. If you click on the application restore button, the top one of the two restore buttons at the top right of the screen, you can make Excel show in a smaller window.

This can be useful when you are running several applications at the same time and you want to transfer between them with the mouse.

Note that the Excel window, which in this case displays an empty and untitled book (Book1), has some areas which have identical functions to those of Word (refer to 'The Word Screen' section in Chapter 3), and other areas which have different functions. Below, we describe only the areas that are exclusive to Excel.

Area	*Function*
Edit line	Contains the selection indicator (cell co-ordinates), and the name box that identifies the selected cell, chart item, or drawing object. The edit line box can display a number, a label, or the formula behind a result.
Cell pointer	Marks the current cell.
Column letter	The letter that identifies each column.
Row number	The number that identifies each row.
Tab scrolling	Clicking on these buttons, scrolls sheet tabs right or left, when there are more tabs than can be displayed at once.
Current sheet	Shows the current sheet amongst a number of sheets in a file. These are named Sheet1, Sheet2, Sheet3, and so on, by default, but can be changed to, say, North, South, East, and West. Clicking on a sheet tab, moves you to that sheet.

| Tab split box | The split box which you drag left to see more of the scroll bar, or right to see more tabs. |
| Drawing Toolbar | The toolbar at the bottom of the screen which can be turned off by using the **View, Toolbars** command and unchecking the **Drawing** option. |

There is an extra split box on Excel's worksheet screen dump, which has not been identified. This is located at the extreme bottom-right corner of the screen, to the left of the 'right horizontal scroll arrow' button. The one identified on the screen dump is located at the extreme right of the screen above the 'top vertical scroll arrow' button. Both of these have to do with splitting the screen; the identified one horizontally, the other vertically. The use of both these split boxes will be discussed later.

Workbook Navigation

When you first enter Excel, the program sets up a series of huge electronic pages, or worksheets, in your computer's memory, many times larger than the small part shown on the screen. Individual cells are identified by column and row location (in that order), with present size extending to 256 columns and 65,536 rows. The columns are labelled from A to Z, followed by AA to AZ, BA to BZ, and so on, to IV, while the rows are numbered from 1 to 65,536.

A worksheet can be thought of as a two-dimensional table made up of rows and columns. The point where a row and column intersect is called a cell, while the reference points of a cell are known as the cell address. The active cell (A1 when you first enter the program) is boxed.

Navigation around the worksheet is achieved by using one of the following keys or key combinations:

- Pressing one of the four arrow keys (→↓←↑) moves the active cell one position right, down, left or up, respectively.

- Pressing the <PgDn> or <PgUp> keys moves the active cell down or up one visible page.

- Pressing the <Ctrl+→> or <Ctrl+↓> key combinations moves the active cell to the extreme right of the worksheet (column IV) or extreme bottom of the worksheet (row 65,536).

- Pressing the <Home> key, moves the active cell to the beginning of a row.

- Pressing the <Ctrl+Home> key combination moves the active cell to the home position, A1.

- Pressing the <Ctrl+End> key combination moves the active cell to the lower right corner of the worksheet's currently used area.

- Pressing the **F5** function key will display the Go To dialogue box shown below.

In the **Go to** box a list of named ranges in the active worksheet (to be discussed shortly) is displayed, or one of the last four references from which you chose the **Go To** command.

In the **Reference** box you type the cell reference or a named range you want to move to.

To move the active cell with a mouse, do the following:

- Point to the cell you want to move to and click the left mouse button. If the cell is not visible, move the window by clicking on the scroll bar arrowhead that points in the direction you want to move,

- To move a page at a time, click in the scroll bar itself.

- For larger moves, drag the box in the scroll bar, but the distances moved will depend on the size of the worksheet.

When you have finished navigating around the worksheet, press the <Ctrl+Home> key combination which will move the active cell to the A1 position (provided you have not fixed titles in any rows or columns or have no hidden rows or columns - more about these later).

Note that the area within which you can move the active cell is referred to as the working area of the worksheet, while the letters and numbers in the border at the top and left of the working area give the 'co-ordinates' of the cells in a worksheet.

The location of the active cell is constantly monitored by the 'selection indicator' which is to be found on the extreme left below the lower Toolbar of the application window. As the active cell is moved, this indicator displays its address, as shown below.

The contents of a cell are displayed above the column letters within what is known as the 'Edit line'. If you type text in the active cell, what you type appears in both the 'Edit line' and the cell itself.

Typing a formula which is preceded by the equals sign (=) to, say, add the contents of three cells, causes the actual formula to appear in the 'Edit line', while the result of the actual calculation appears in the active cell when the <Enter> key is pressed.

Moving Between Sheets:

You can scroll between sheets by clicking one of the arrows situated to the left of Sheet 1, as shown below. We have labelled these as 'Tab scrolling buttons'. The inner arrows scroll sheets one at a time in the direction of the arrow, while the outer arrows scroll to the end, or beginning, of the group of available sheets. A sheet is then made current by clicking its tab.

With the keyboard, you can scroll one sheet at a time, and make it active at the same time, by using the <Ctrl+PgDn> key combination. Using <Ctrl+PgUp> scrolls in the reverse direction.

To display more sheet tabs at a time, drag the split box to the right. The reverse action displays less sheet tabs. To rename sheets, double-click at their tab, then type a new name to replace the highlighted name of the particular sheet tab.

To insert a sheet in front of a certain sheet, make that sheet current, then use the **Insert, Worksheet** command sequence. To delete a sheet, make it current and use the **Edit, Delete Sheet** command sequence.

102

Rearranging Sheet Order:

If you need to rearrange the order in which sheets are being held in a workbook, you can do so by dragging a particular sheet to its new position, as shown below.

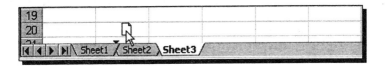

While you are dragging the tab of the sheet you want to move, the mouse pointer changes to an arrow pointing to a sheet. The small solid arrowhead to the left of the mouse pointer indicates the place where the sheet you are moving will be placed.

Grouping Worksheets:

You can select several sheets to group them together so that data entry, editing, or formatting can be made easier and more consistent.

To select adjacent sheets, click the first sheet tab, hold down the <Shift> key and then click the last sheet tab in the group. To select non-adjacent sheets, click the first sheet tab, hold down the <Ctrl> key and then click the other sheet tabs you want to group together.

Selecting sheets in the above manner, causes the word '[Group]' to appear in the Title bar of the active window, and the tabs of the selected sheets to be shown in white. To cancel the selection, click at the tab of any sheet which is not part of the selected group.

Selecting a Range of Cells:

To select a range of cells, say, A3:C3, point to cell A3, then

- press the left mouse button, and while holding it pressed, drag the mouse to the right.

To select a range from the keyboard, first make active the first cell in the range, then

- hold down the <Shift> key and use the right arrow key (→) to highlight the required range.

To select a 3D range, across several sheets, select the range in the first sheet, then

- release the mouse button, hold down the <Shift> key, and click the Tab of the last sheet in the range.

Shortcut Menus:

While a range of cells in a sheet is selected, or a group of sheets is active, you can access a shortcut menu of relevant commands by pressing the right mouse button. This produces a shortcut menu, as shown here, of the most common commands relevant to what you are doing at the time.

Viewing Multiple Workbook Sheets

To see more clearly what you are doing when working with multiple workbook sheets, type the text '1st' in location A1 of Sheet1, the text '2nd' in Sheet2, and so on. Then use the **Window, New Window** command to add three extra windows to your worksheet (to add extra sheets in a workbook, use the **Insert, Worksheet** command). Finally, use the **Window, Arrange, Tiled** command to display the four sheets as shown below.

To move from one window to another, simply point with the mouse to the cell of the window you want to go to and click the left mouse button. To display a different sheet in each window, go to a window and click the sheet's tab.

To return to single-window view mode from a tiled or cascade mode, click the maximise button of the active window.

Entering Information

We will now investigate how information can be entered into a worksheet. But first, make sure you are in Sheet1, then return to the Home (A1) position, by pressing the <Ctrl+Home> key combination, then type the words:

```
PROJECT ANALYSIS
```

As you type, the characters appear in both the 'Edit line' and the active cell. If you make a mistake, press the <BkSp> key to erase the previous letter or the <Esc> key to start again. When you have finished, press <Enter>.

Note that what you have just typed in has been entered in cell A1, even though the whole of the word ANALYSIS appears to be in cell B1. If you use the right arrow key to move the active cell to B1 you will see that the cell is indeed empty.

Typing any letter at the beginning of an entry into a cell results in a 'text' entry being formed automatically, otherwise known as a 'label'. If the length of the text is longer than the width of a cell, it will continue into the next cell to the right of the current active cell, provided that cell is empty, otherwise the displayed information will be truncated.

To edit information already in a cell, either

• double-click the cell in question, or

• make that cell the active cell and press the **F2** function key.

The cursor keys, the <Home> and <End> keys, as well as the <Ins> and <Del> keys can be used to move the cursor and/or edit information as required.

 You can also 'undo' the last 16 actions carried out since the program was last in the **Ready** mode, by either using the **Edit, Undo Entry** command or clicking the Undo button.

Next, move the active cell to B3 and type

    Jan

Pressing the right arrow key (→) will automatically enter the typed information into the cell and also move the active cell one cell to the right, in this case to C3. Now type

    Feb

and press <Enter>.

The looks of a worksheet can be enhanced somewhat by using different types of borders around specific cells. To do this, first select the range of cells, then click at the down arrow of the Borders icon on the Formatting Toolbar, shown here, which displays twelve different types of borders, as shown below.

In our example, we have selected the cell range A3:C3, then we chose the 8th border from the display table.

Next, move to cell A4 and type the label Income, then enter the numbers 14000 and 15000 in cells B4 and C4, respectively, as shown below, but note that by default the labels 'Jan' and 'Feb' are left justified, while the numbers are right justified.

	A	B	C	D	E	F	G	H
1	PROJECT ANALYSIS							
2								
3		Jan	Feb					
4	Income	14000	15000		✥			
5								

Changing Text Alignment and Fonts:

One way of improving the looks of this worksheet is to also right justify the text 'Jan' and 'Feb' within their respective cells. To do this, move the active cell to B3 and select the range B3 to C3 by dragging the mouse, then either click the 'Align Right' icon, shown here, or choose the

Format, Cells

command, then select the **Alignment** tab from the displayed Format Cells dialogue box, shown below, click the down-arrow against the **Horizontal** text box, highlight **Right** from the drop-down menu options, and press **OK**.

No matter which method you choose, the text should now appear right justified within their cells. However, although the latter method is lengthier, it nevertheless provides you with greater flexibility in displaying text, both in terms of position and orientation.

We could further improve the looks of our worksheet by choosing a different font for the heading 'Project Analysis'. To achieve this, select cell A1, then click on the 'Font Size' button on the second Toolbar, to reveal the band of available point sizes for the selected font, as shown overleaf. From this band, choose 14, then click in succession the 'Bold' and 'Italic' icons.

Finally, since the numbers in cells B4 to C4 represent money, it would be better if these were prefixed with the £ sign. To do this, select the cell range B4:C4, then either click the 'Currency Style' button on the second Toolbar, shown here, or choose the

F̲ormat, S̲tyle

command and select **Currency** from the list under **S̲tyle Name** in the displayed Style dialogue box.

The numbers within the chosen range will now be displayed in currency form, provided the width of the cells is sufficient to accommodate them. In our example, the entered numbers are far too long to fit in currency form in the default cell width and appear as shown under the 'Feb' entry.

To see the actual numbers, we must increase the width of the columns B4:C4 to 11 characters wide (as shown at the top right of the display within a pop-up text box). To do this, place the mouse pointer in between the column letters on the dividing line, and drag the pointer to the right, as pointed to above, until the width of the column is displayed as 11.00.

Saving a Workbook

Now, let us assume that we would like to stop at this point, but would also like to save the work entered so far before leaving the program. First, return to the Home position by pressing <Ctrl+Home>. This is good practice because when a workbook is opened later, the position of the cell pointer at the time of saving the file appears at the top left corner of the opened worksheet, which might cause confusion if below and to the right of it there are no entries - you might think that you have opened an empty worksheet.

Next, choose the **File, Save** command to reveal the Save As dialogue box. You could select to save your work in the default **My Documents** folder, or on a floppy disc in the **a:** drive as we have done - the choice is yours. Next, type the new name of the file, say, **Project 1** in the **File name** box. The file will be saved in the default file type *Microsoft Excel Workbook*, as displayed in the **Save as type** box. Excel adds the file extension **.xls** automatically and uses it to identify it, but normally you cannot see it.

If you want to create backup files or provide password protection to your file, click the **Options** button. Clicking the **Save** button, causes the file to be saved under the chosen name.

Opening a Workbook

An already saved workbook, or file, can be opened by
 either clicking at the 'Open' icon, shown here,
or selecting the

File, Open

command which displays the Open dialogue box. Do
not forget to change the drive to **a:**, if that is where you
saved your work (by selecting 3½ Floppy (A:) in the
Look in box drop-down list). Excel asks for a filename
to open, with the default *Microsoft Excel Files* being
displayed in the **Files of type** box, as shown below. If
the file was saved, select it by clicking its name in the
list box, then click the **Open** button.

Open			? ☒
Look in:	3½ Floppy (A:)		

Project 1.xls

Open
Cancel
Advanced...

Find files that match these search criteria:
File name:
Files of type: Microsoft Excel Files (*.xl*; *.xls; *.xla)
Text or property:
Last modified: any time

Find Now
New Search

1 file(s) found.

If you haven't saved it, don't worry as you could just as
easily start afresh.

If you want to change the logged drive, click the
down-arrow against the **Look in** box, and select the
appropriate drive from the drop-down list.

Exiting Excel

To exit Excel, close any displayed dialogue boxes by clicking the **Cancel** button, and make sure that the word **Ready** is displayed on the status bar (press the <Esc> key until it does), and either

- choose the **File, Exit** command,
- use the <Alt+F4> key combination, or
- click the Close button.

No matter which command you choose, if you have changed any opened worksheet, Excel will warn you and will ask for confirmation before exiting the program.

7. FILLING IN A WORKSHEET

We will use, as an example on how a worksheet can be built up, the few entries on 'Project Analysis' from the previous chapter. If you have saved **Project 1**, then either click the Open button, or use the **File, Open** command, then highlight its filename in the Open dialogue box, and click the **OK** button. If you haven't saved it, don't worry as you could just as easily start afresh.

Next, either double-click the contents of a cell to edit existing entries, or simply retype the contents of cells, so that your worksheet looks as near as possible to the one below. For formatting details, see below and the next page.

X Microsoft Excel - Project 2.xls

File Edit View Insert Format Tools Data Window Help

Arial ... 10 ...

F8

	A	B	C	D	E	F	G	H
1	**PROJECT ANALYSIS: ADEPT CONSULTANTS LTD**							
2								
3		Jan	Feb	Mar	1st Quarter			
4	Income	£ 14,000.00	£15,000.00	£ 16,000.00	£ 45,000.00			
5	Costs:							
6	Wages	2000	3000	4000				
7	Travel	400	500	600				
8	Rent	300	300	300				
9	Heat/Light	150	200	130				
10	Phone/Fax	250	300	350				
11	Adverts	1100	1200	1300				
12	Total Costs							
13	Profit							
14	Cumulative							
15								

The lines, like the double line stretching from A3 to E3 were entered by first selecting the cell range A3:E3, then clicking the down-arrow of the 'Borders' icon on the second Toolbar, and selecting the appropriate border from the 12 displayed options.

Formatting Entries

The information in cell A1 (PROJECT ANALYSIS: ADEPT CONSULTANTS LTD) was entered left justified and formatted by clicking on the 'Font Size' button on the Formatting Toolbar, and selecting 14 point font size from the band of available font sizes, then clicking in succession the 'Bold' and 'Italic' icons.

The text in the cell block B3:E3 was formatted by first selecting the range and then clicking the 'Centre' alignment icon on the second Toolbar, so the text within the range was displayed centre justified.

The numbers within the cell block B4:E4 were formatted by first selecting the range, then clicking the 'Currency Style' icon on the second Toolbar, shown here, so the numbers appeared with two digits after the decimal point and prefixed with the £ sign.

All the text appearing in column A (apart from that in cell A1) was just typed in (left justified), as shown in the screen dump on the previous page.

Filling a Range by Example:

To fill a range by example, select the range, point at 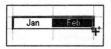 the bottom right corner of the selected range and when the mouse pointer changes to a small cross, drag the mouse in the required direction.

In the above case, the next cell to the right will automatically fill with the text 'Mar' (Excel anticipates that you want to fill cells by example with the abbreviations for months, and does it for you). Not only that, but it also copies the format of the selected range forward. It is, therefore, evident that selecting ranges and using icons makes various tasks a lot easier.

Entering Text, Numbers and Formulae:

Excel 97 allows you to format both text (labels) and numbers in any way you choose. For example, you can have numbers centre justified in their cells.

When text, a number, a formula, or an Excel function is entered into a cell, or reference is made to the contents of a cell by the cell address, then the content of the status bar changes from **Ready** to **Enter**. This status can be changed back to **Ready** by either completing an entry and pressing <Enter> or one of the arrow keys, or by pressing <Esc>.

We can find the 1st quarter total income from consultancy, by activating cell E4, typing

=B4+C4+D4

and pressing <Enter>. The total first quarter income is added, using the above formula, and the result is placed in cell E4.

Now complete the insertion into the spreadsheet of the various amounts under 'costs' and then choose the

File, Save As

command to save the resultant worksheet under the filename **Project 2**, before going on any further. Remember that saving your work on disc often enough is a good thing to get used to, as even the shortest power cut can cause the loss of hours of hard work!

Using Functions

In our example, writing a formula that adds the contents of three columns is not too difficult or lengthy a task. But imagine having to add 20 columns! For this reason Excel has an in-built summation function which can be used to add any number of columns (or rows).

To illustrate how this and other functions can be used, activate cell E4 and press the Paste Function button shown here. If the function you require appears on the displayed dialogue box under **Function name**, choose it, otherwise select the appropriate class from the list under **Function category**.

Choosing the **SUM** function, inserts the entry SUM(B4:D4) in the Edit line, as shown below. Clicking the **OK** button, causes this function to be pasted into cell E4, adding all the numbers in the range.

Using the AutoSum Icon:

With addition, there is a better and quicker way of letting Excel work out the desired result. To illustrate this, select the cell range B6:E12, which contains the 'Costs' we would like to add up. To add these in both the horizontal and vertical direction, we include in the selected range an empty column to the right of the numbers and an empty row below the numbers, as shown below.

	A	B	C	D	E	F	G	H
1	PROJECT ANALYSIS: ADEPT CONSULTANTS LTD							
2								
3		Jan	Feb	Mar	1st Quarter			
4	Income	£ 14,000.00	£15,000.00	£ 16,000.00	£ 45,000.00			
5	Costs:							
6	Wages	2000	3000	4000				
7	Travel	400	500	600				
8	Rent	300	300	300				
9	Heat/Light	150	200	130				
10	Phone/Fax	250	300	350				
11	Adverts	1100	1200	1300				
12	Total Costs							

Pressing the 'AutoSum' icon, shown here, inserts the result of the summations in the empty column and row, as shown below. The selected range remains selected so that any other formatting can be applied by simply pressing the appropriate icon button.

	A	B	C	D	E	F	G	H
1	PROJECT ANALYSIS: ADEPT CONSULTANTS LTD							
2								
3		Jan	Feb	Mar	1st Quarter			
4	Income	£ 14,000.00	£15,000.00	£ 16,000.00	£ 45,000.00			
5	Costs:							
6	Wages	2000	3000	4000	9000			
7	Travel	400	500	600	1500			
8	Rent	300	300	300	900			
9	Heat/Light	150	200	130	480			
10	Phone/Fax	250	300	350	900			
11	Adverts	1100	1200	1300	3600			
12	Total Costs	4200	5500	6680	16380			

Now complete the insertion of formulae in the rest of the worksheet, noting that 'Profit', in B13, is the difference between 'Income' and 'Total Cost', calculated by the formula **=B4-B12**. To complete the entry, this formula should be copied using the 'fill by example' method into the three cells to its right.

The 'Cumulative' entry in cell B14 should be a simple reference to cell B13, that is **=B13**, while in cell C14 it should be **=B14+C13**. Similarly, the latter formula is copied into cell D14 using the 'fill by example' method.

Next, format the entire range B6:E12 by selecting the range and clicking the 'Currency' button.

If you make any mistakes and copy formats or information into cells you did not mean to, use the

Edit, Underline

command or click the Undo button which allows you to selectively undo what you were just doing. To blank the contents within a range of cells, first select the range, then press the <Del> key.

The worksheet, up to this point, should look as follows:

	A	B	C	D	E	F	G	H
1	**PROJECT ANALYSIS: ADEPT CONSULTANTS LTD**							
2								
3		Jan	Feb	Mar	1st Quarter			
4	Income	£ 14,000.00	£15,000.00	£ 16,000.00	£ 45,000.00			
5	Costs:							
6	Wages	£ 2,000.00	£ 3,000.00	£ 4,000.00	£ 9,000.00			
7	Travel	£ 400.00	£ 500.00	£ 600.00	£ 1,500.00			
8	Rent	£ 300.00	£ 300.00	£ 300.00	£ 900.00			
9	Heat/Light	£ 150.00	£ 200.00	£ 130.00	£ 480.00			
10	Phone/Fax	£ 250.00	£ 300.00	£ 350.00	£ 900.00			
11	Adverts	£ 1,100.00	£ 1,200.00	£ 1,300.00	£ 3,600.00			
12	Total Costs	£ 4,200.00	£ 5,500.00	£ 6,680.00	£ 16,380.00			
13	Profit	£ 9,800.00	£ 9,500.00	£ 9,320.00	£ 28,620.00			
14	Cumulative	£ 9,800.00	£19,300.00	£ 28,620.00				
15								

Finally, use the **File, Save As** command to save your work under the filename **Project 3**.

Printing a Worksheet

To print a worksheet, make sure that the printer you propose to use was defined when you first installed Windows.

If you have named more than one printer in your original installation of Windows, and want to select a printer other than your original first choice, then select the **File, Print** command, click the down-arrow against the **Name** box on the displayed Print dialogue box and select the required printer, as shown below.

If you want to change the paper size, print orientation or printer resolution, click the **Properties** button on the Print dialogue box. These and other changes to the appearance of the printout can also be made by choosing the **File, Page Setup** command which causes the Page Setup dialogue box to be displayed, as shown overleaf.

![Page Setup dialogue box showing Page tab with Orientation (Portrait/Landscape), Scaling options (Adjust to: 100% normal size, Fit to: 1 page(s) wide by 1 tall), Paper size: A4 (210 x 297 mm), Print quality: High, First page number: Auto, and buttons for Print..., Print Preview, Options..., OK, Cancel]

By selecting the appropriate Tab on this dialogue box, you can change your **Page** settings, page **Margins**, specify a **Header/Footer**, and control how a **Sheet** should be printed. Each Tab displays a different dialogue box, appropriate to the function at hand. In the **Header/Footer** dialogue box you can even click the down-arrow against the Header and Footer boxes to display a suggested list for these, appropriate to the work you are doing, the person responsible for it and even the date it is being carried out! Try it.

A very useful feature of Excel is the **Scaling** facility shown in the above dialogue box. You can print actual size or a percentage of it, or you can choose to fit your worksheet on to one page which allows Excel to scale your work automatically.

To preview a worksheet, click the 'Print Preview' icon on the Toolbar, shown here, or click the **Print Preview** button on the Page Setup dialogue box, or the **Preview** button on the Print dialogue box. You can even use the **File, Print Preview** command!

The idea of all these preview choices is to make it easy for you to see your work on screen before committing it to paper, thus saving a few more trees!

120

Enhancing a Worksheet

You can make your work look more professional by adopting various enhancements, such as single and double line cell borders, shading certain cells, and adding meaningful headers and footers.

However, with Excel you can easily select a pre-defined style to display your work on both the screen and on paper. To do this, place the active cell within the table (or range) you want to format, say C5, then select the **Format, AutoFormat** which will cause the following dialogue box to appear on the screen, displaying a sample of the chosen table format. In this way you can choose what best suits your needs. We selected 'Classic 2' and pressed **OK**.

Next, reduce the title of the worksheet to PROJECT ANALYSIS, then centre it within the range A1:E1, by first selecting the range, then clicking the 'Merge and Centre' icon, shown here, which causes the title to centre within the specified range.

Finally, save the worksheet as **Project 4**, before going on.

121

Header and Footer Icons and Codes:

With the help of header and footer icons and their codes, shown below, you can position text or automatically insert information at the top or bottom of a report printout.

To add a header to our printed example, use the **File, Page Setup** command and click first the **Header/Footer** Tab, then the **Custom Header** button and type the information displayed below in the **Left section** and **Right section** of the Header box.

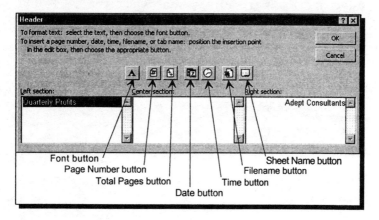

While the insertion pointer is in, say, the **Centre section** of the Header box, pointing and clicking on the 'Sheet Name' button, inserts the &[Tab] code which has the effect of inserting the sheet name of the current active sheet at the time of printing. The first icon button displays the Font dialogue box, while the others display the following codes:

Code	Action
&[Page]	Inserts a page number.
&[Pages]	Inserts the total number of pages.
&[Date]	Inserts the current date.
&[Time]	Inserts the current time.
&[File]	Inserts the filename of the current workbook.

Setting a Print Area:

To choose a smaller print area than the current worksheet, select the required area by highlighting the starting cell of the area and dragging the mouse, or using the **<Shift+Arrows>**, to highlight the block, and use the **File, Print** command which displays the following dialogue box:

Choose the **Selection** button in the **Print What** box, and either click the **Preview** or the **OK** button to preview your report on screen or print it on paper. Once in preview mode, the following icons are available to you.

The first two allow you to change sheets, while the next one allows you to review your print output magnified or at full page size - when in full page size, the mouse pointer looks like a magnifying glass, as above. The next four icons can be used to print, change page settings, display and change the margins, or adjust the page size by dragging the page breaks to a new position. To return to normal view, click the **Close** button.

Another way to set the area to print is using the **File, Print Area, Set Print Area** menu command. To print selected sheets or the entire workbook, click the appropriate button in the **Print What** box of the Print dialogue box.

The default selection in the **Print What** box is **Active sheet(s)** which is also what will be printed out if you

click the 'Print' icon, shown here. If you have included headers and footers, these will be printed out irrespective of whether you choose to print a selected range or a selected worksheet. To centre the page horizontally on the paper, use the **File, Page Setup** command, click the Margins tab and select the option. Finally, printing our worksheet, produces the following page:

Quarterly Profits   Adept Consultants

	Jan	Feb	Mar	1st Quarter
Income	£ 14,000.00	£ 15,000.00	£ 16,000.00	£ 45,000.00
Costs:				
Wages	£ 2,000.00	£ 3,000.00	£ 4,000.00	£ 9,000.00
Travel	£ 400.00	£ 500.00	£ 600.00	£ 1,500.00
Rent	£ 300.00	£ 300.00	£ 300.00	£ 900.00
Heat/Light	£ 150.00	£ 200.00	£ 130.00	£ 480.00
Phone/Fax	£ 250.00	£ 300.00	£ 350.00	£ 900.00
Adverts	£ 1,100.00	£ 1,200.00	£ 1,300.00	£ 3,600.00
Total Costs	£ 4,200.00	£ 5,500.00	£ 6,680.00	£ 16,380.00
Profit	£ 9,800.00	£ 9,500.00	£ 9,320.00	£ 28,620.00
Cumulative	£ 9,800.00	£ 19,300.00	£ 28,620.00	

5/1/96   Page 1

3-Dimensional Worksheets

In Excel 97, a Workbook is a 3-dimensional file made up with a series of flat 2-dimensional sheets stacked 'on top of each other'. Each sheet is the same size, and in itself, behaves the same as the more ordinary worksheets. As mentioned previously, each separate sheet in a file has its own Tab identifier at the bottom of the screen. Ranges can be set to span several different sheets to build up 3-dimensional blocks of data. These blocks can then be manipulated, copied, or moved to other locations in the file. A cell can reference any other cell in the file, no matter what sheet it is on, and an extended range of functions can be used to process these 3-dimensional ranges.

Manipulating Ranges:

The best way to demonstrate a new idea is to work through an example - we will use the worksheet saved under **Project 4**. Next, start Excel, use the **File, Open** command, or click the File Open icon, and select **Project 4**. On pressing <Enter>, the worksheet is displayed on the screen as shown on the facing page.

Copying Sheets in a Workbook:

We will now fill another three sheets behind the present one, in order to include information about ADEPT Consultants' trading during the other three quarters of the year. The easiest way of doing this is by copying the information in Sheet1, including the formatting and the entered formulae, onto the other three sheets, then edit the numerical information in these appropriately.

To simplify this operation, Excel has a facility which allows you to copy a sheet into a workbook. There are two ways of doing this: (a) with the mouse, or (b) using the menus.

125

With the mouse, make the sheet you want to copy the current sheet, then press the <Ctrl> key, and while keeping it pressed, point with the mouse on the Tab of Sheet1 and drag it to the right, as follows:

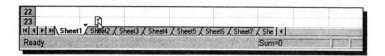

A small black triangle indicates the place where the copy will be inserted. If you insert a copy, say before Sheet2, when you release the mouse button the inserted sheet will be given the name Sheet1(2), as shown above, where we are about to insert a second copy before Sheet2 which will be named Sheet1(3).

To copy a sheet with the menus, select the **Edit, Move or Copy Sheet** command, then highlight Sheet2

in the **Before sheet** list of the displayed dialogue box, then check the **Create a copy** option at the bottom of the dialogue box, and press the **OK** button. Sheet1(2) will be inserted in the Workbook, in the above case.

When you have three copies placed, double-click the Tabs of Sheet1 and the three new sheets and change their names to 'Quarter 1', 'Quarter 2', 'Quarter 3' and 'Quarter 4', respectively. The contents of the second sheet should be as follows:

	A	B	C	D	E	F
1	**PROJECT ANALYSIS 2nd Quarter**					
2						
3		Apr	May	Jun	2nd Quarter	
4	Income	£15,500.00	£16,000.00	£16,500.00	£48,000.00	
5	Costs:					
6	Wages	£ 3,500.00	£ 4,000.00	£ 4,500.00	£12,000.00	
7	Travel	£ 500.00	£ 550.00	£ 580.00	£ 1,630.00	
8	Rent	£ 300.00	£ 300.00	£ 300.00	£ 900.00	
9	Heat/Light	£ 150.00	£ 120.00	£ 100.00	£ 370.00	
10	Phone/Fax	£ 300.00	£ 350.00	£ 400.00	£ 1,050.00	
11	Adverts	£ 1,250.00	£ 1,300.00	£ 1,350.00	£ 3,900.00	
12	Total Costs	£ 6,000.00	£ 6,620.00	£ 7,230.00	£19,850.00	
13	*Profit*	£ 9,500.00	£ 9,380.00	£ 9,270.00	£28,150.00	
14	*Cumulative*	£ 9,500.00	£18,880.00	£28,150.00		
15						
16						
17						
18						

Quarter 1 \ **Quarter 2** / Quarter 3 / Quarter 4 / Sheet2

The easiest way to enter these 2nd Quarter results is to edit the copied data (from Quarter 1) by either using the EDIT key (**F2**), or double-clicking the cell you want to edit. You should now be in a position to complete editing this sheet. Be extra careful, from now on, to check the identification Tab at the bottom of the screen, so as not to get the sheets mixed up. You do not want to spend time editing the wrong worksheet!

After building up the four worksheets (one for each quarter - see below for details on the 3rd and 4th quarters) save the file as **Project 5**.

	Jul	Aug	Sep	Oct	Nov	Dec
Income	17,000	17,500	18,000	18,500	19,000	19,500
Costs:						
Wages	4,000	4,500	5,000	4,500	5,000	5,500
Travel	600	650	680	630	670	700
Rent	300	300	300	300	300	300
Heat/Light	50	80	120	160	200	250
Phone/Fax	350	380	420	400	420	450
Adverts	1,400	1,450	1,500	1,480	1,500	1,530

Linking Sheets

A consolidation sheet could be placed in front of our 'stack' of data sheets to show a full year's results, by making a copy of the 1st Quarter sheet and placing it in front of it. Next, delete the entries in columns B to E, and name it 'Consolidation'.

We are now in a position to link the consolidation sheet to the other quarterly data sheets so that the information contained on them is automatically summarised and updated on it. The quarter totals in columns E of sheets Quarter 1, Quarter 2, Quarter 3, and Quarter 4, can be copied in turn to the clipboard using the **Edit, Copy** command, and then pasted to the appropriate column of the Consolidation sheet with the use of the **Edit, Paste Special** command and clicking the **Paste Link** button on the displayed dialogue box.

Note: Empty cells linked with this method, like those in cells E5 of each quarter, appear as 0 (zero) in the Consolidation sheet, and cannot be removed. To correct this, copy each column E of each quarter in two stages; E3:E4, then E6:E13.

Next, insert appropriate formulae in row 14 to correctly calculate the cumulative values in the Consolidation sheet. The result should be as follows:

	E13	▼	=	(='Quarter 4'!$E$6:$E$13)				
	A	B	C	D	E	F	G	H
1		**PROJECT ANALYSIS - Year Summary**						
2								
3		1st Quarter	2nd Quarter	3rd Quarter	4th Quarter			
4	Income	£ 45,000.00	£ 48,000.00	£ 52,500.00	£ 57,000.00			
5	Costs:							
6	Wages	£ 9,000.00	£ 12,000.00	£ 13,500.00	£ 15,000.00			
7	Travel	£ 1,500.00	£ 1,630.00	£ 1,930.00	£ 2,000.00			
8	Rent	£ 900.00	£ 900.00	£ 900.00	£ 900.00			
9	Heat/Light	£ 480.00	£ 370.00	£ 250.00	£ 610.00			
10	Phone/Fax	£ 900.00	£ 1,050.00	£ 1,150.00	£ 1,270.00			
11	Adverts	£ 3,600.00	£ 3,900.00	£ 4,350.00	£ 4,510.00			
12	Total Costs	£ 16,380.00	£ 19,850.00	£ 22,080.00	£ 24,290.00			
13	*Profit*	£ 28,620.00	£ 28,150.00	£ 30,420.00	£ 32,710.00			
14	*Cumulative*	£ 28,620.00	£ 56,770.00	£ 87,190.00	£119,900.00			

Finally, save the resultant workbook as **Project 6**.

Relative and Absolute Cell Addresses

Entering a mathematical expression into Excel, such as the formula in cell C14 which was

    =B14+C13

causes Excel to interpret it as 'add the contents of cell one column to the left of the current position, to the contents of cell one row above the current position'. In this way, when the formula was later copied into cell address D14, the contents of the cell relative to the left position of D14 (i.e. C14) and the contents of the cell one row above it (i.e. D13) were used, instead of the original cell addresses entered in C14. This is relative addressing.

To see the effect of relative versus absolute addressing, copy the formula in cell C14 into C17, as shown below:

	C17	▼	=	=B17+C16		
	A	B	C	D	E	F
1	*PROJECT ANALYSIS - Year Summary*					
2						
3		1st Quarter	2nd Quarter	3rd Quarter	4th Quarter	
4	Income	£ 45,000.00	£ 48,000.00	£ 52,500.00	£ 57,000.00	
5	Costs:					
6	Wages	£ 9,000.00	£ 12,000.00	£ 13,500.00	£ 15,000.00	
7	Travel	£ 1,500.00	£ 1,630.00	£ 1,930.00	£ 2,000.00	
8	Rent	£ 900.00	£ 900.00	£ 900.00	£ 900.00	
9	Heat/Light	£ 480.00	£ 370.00	£ 250.00	£ 610.00	
10	Phone/Fax	£ 900.00	£ 1,050.00	£ 1,150.00	£ 1,270.00	
11	Adverts	£ 3,600.00	£ 3,900.00	£ 4,350.00	£ 4,510.00	
12	Total Costs	£ 16,380.00	£ 19,850.00	£ 22,080.00	£ 24,290.00	
13	*Profit*	£ 28,620.00	£ 28,150.00	£ 30,420.00	£ 32,710.00	
14	*Cumulative*	£ 28,620.00	£ 56,770.00	£ 87,190.00	£119,900.00	
15						
16						
17			£ -	⊕		

Note that in cell C14 the formula was =B14+C13. However, when copied into cell C17 the formula appears as

=B17+C16

because it has been interpreted as relative addressing. In this case, no value appears in cell C17 because we are attempting to add two blank cells.

Now change the formula in C14 by editing it to

=$B$14+$C$13

which is interpreted as absolute addressing. Copying this formula into cell C17 calculates the correct result. Highlight cell C17 and observe the cell references in its formula; they have not changed from those of cell C14.

The $ sign must prefix both the column reference and the row reference. Mixed cell addressing is permitted; as for example when a column address reference is needed to be taken as absolute, while a row address reference is needed to be taken as relative. In such a case, the column letter is prefixed by the $ sign.

When building an absolute cell reference in a formula, it is easier to select the cell with the mouse pointer and keep pressing the **F4** key until the correct $ prefix is set.

Freezing Panes on Screen

Sometimes there might be too much information on screen and attempting to see a certain part of a sheet might cause the labels associated with that information to scroll off the screen.

To freeze column (or row) labels of a worksheet on screen, move the cell pointer to the right (or below) the column (or row) which you want to freeze, and use the **Window, Freeze Panes** command. Everything to the left of (or above) the cell pointer will freeze on the screen.

To unfreeze panes, use the **Window, Unfreeze Panes** command.

8. SPREADSHEET CHARTS

Excel allows information within a worksheet to be represented in graphical form, which makes data more accessible to non-expert users who might not be familiar with the spreadsheet format. The saying 'a picture is worth a thousand words', applies equally well to charts and figures.

The package allows the use of several chart and graph types, including area, bar, column, line, doughnut, radar, XY, pie, combination, and several 3-D options of these charts. In all, Excel allows fourteen different types of charts, with almost 100 pre-defined formats, which can be selected by using the appropriate icon. These are made available to you once you have selected the data you want to chart and clicked on the Chart Wizard button on the toolbar.

Charts (you can have several per worksheet) can be displayed on screen at the same time as the worksheet from which they were derived, since they appear in their own 'chart' frame and can be embedded anywhere on a worksheet. Furthermore, they can be sent to an appropriate output device, such as a plotter or printer. Although this charting module rivals a standalone graphics package, and one could write a separate book on it, an attempt will be made to present its basics, in the space available within this book.

Preparing for a Column Chart

In order to illustrate some of the graphing capabilities of Excel, we will now plot the income of the consulting company we discussed in the **Project 6** file. However, before we can go on, you will need to complete the entries for the last two quarters of trading of the Adept Consultants' example, if you haven't already done so - see end of previous chapter.

Next, link the quarterly totals to the consolidation sheet, calculate the year's total, as shown below, and save the resultant workbook as **Project 7**, before going on.

F4		= =SUM(B4:E4)				
	A	B	C	D	E	F	G
1		*PROJECT ANALYSIS - Year Summary*					
2							
3		1st Quarter	2nd Quarter	3rd Quarter	4th Quarter	Total	
4	Income	£ 45,000.00	£ 48,000.00	£ 52,500.00	£ 57,000.00	£ 202,500.00	
5	Costs:						
6	Wages	£ 9,000.00	£ 12,000.00	£ 13,500.00	£ 15,000.00	£ 49,500.00	
7	Travel	£ 1,500.00	£ 1,630.00	£ 1,930.00	£ 2,000.00	£ 7,060.00	
8	Rent	£ 900.00	£ 900.00	£ 900.00	£ 900.00	£ 3,600.00	
9	Heat/Light	£ 480.00	£ 370.00	£ 250.00	£ 610.00	£ 1,710.00	
10	Phone/Fax	£ 900.00	£ 1,050.00	£ 1,150.00	£ 1,270.00	£ 4,370.00	
11	Adverts	£ 3,600.00	£ 3,900.00	£ 4,350.00	£ 4,510.00	£ 16,360.00	
12	Total Costs	£ 16,380.00	£ 19,850.00	£ 22,080.00	£ 24,290.00	£ 82,600.00	
13	Profit	£ 28,620.00	£ 28,150.00	£ 30,420.00	£ 32,710.00	£ 119,900.00	
14	Cumulative	£ 28,620.00	£ 56,770.00	£ 87,190.00	£ 119,900.00		
15							

`|◄ ◄ ► ►| \ Consolidation / Quarter 1 / Quarter 2 / Quarter 3 / Quar ◄ |`

Now we need to select the range of the data we want to graph. The range of data to be graphed in Excel does not have to be contiguous for each graph, as with some other spreadsheets. With Excel, you select your data from different parts of a sheet with the <Ctrl> key pressed down. This method has the advantage of automatic recalculation should any changes be made to the original data. You could also collect data from different sheets to one 'graphing' sheet by linking them as we did with the consolidation sheet.

If you don't want the chart to be recalculated when you do this, then you must use the **Edit, Copy** and **Edit, Paste Special** commands and choose the **Values** option from the displayed dialogue box, which copies a selected range to a specified target area of the worksheet and converts formulae to values. This is necessary, as cells containing formulae cannot be pasted directly since it would cause the relative cell addresses to adjust to the new locations; each formula would then recalculate a new value for each cell and give wrong results.

132

The Chart Wizard

To obtain a chart of 'Income' versus 'Quarters', select
the data in cell range A3..E4, then either click
the Chart Wizard button, shown here, or use
the **Insert, Chart** command. The Chart Wizard
then opens the first of four dialogue boxes, as
shown below, which guide you through the process.

Now select the 3-D Column type and click the **Next >**
button at the bottom of the displayed Chart Wizard
dialogue box (not shown above). The second dialogue
box is then displayed as follows, after clicking the
Columns radio button pointed to below.

133

The third Chart Wizard dialogue box allows you to give a title to your chart and annotate the x- and y-axes, while the fourth dialogue box allows you to place the chart either on a separate sheet or on the sheet that was active when you first started the charting process. On pressing the **Finish** button the following chart should appear on your worksheet.

Note that to find out the exact details of a given column on a chart, you need only place the mouse pointer on it to cause a banner to appear with the desired information.

While the frame containing a chart is selected (you can tell from the presence of the small black squares around it), you can change its size by dragging the small two-headed arrow pointer (which appears when the mouse pointer is placed on the small black squares of the frame). You can also move the frame and its contents to another position on the worksheet by pointing to the chart area, pressing and keeping depressed the left mouse button until the pointer changes to a small four-headed arrow shape, then dragging the changed mouse pointer to a new position.

As an example of what you can do with a chart, let us first select it, then either double-click within the chart area or use the **Format, Selected Chart Area** command to obtain the following dialogue box:

From this dialogue box you can choose a pattern to be used as a frame, by selecting **Custom** under the Patterns tab and choose the 7th **Style**, the 4th **Weight** line, check the **Shadow** box and press **OK**.

Try it, then change the first quarter income from £45,000 to £55,000 (on the Quarter 1 sheet), and watch how the change is reflected on the redrawn graph on the Consolidation sheet displayed below.

You can change the type of chart shown on screen by first selecting it, then using the **Chart, Chart Type** command to display the first Chart Wizard dialogue box.

Finally, revert to the original entry for the first quarter's income, change your chart back to a simple column type, and then save your work again under the filename **Project 7** by simply pressing the Save icon shown here. Your current work will be saved to disc replacing the previous version under the same filename.

When Excel creates a chart, it plots each row or column of data in the selected range as a 'data series', such as a group of bars, lines, etc. A chart can contain many data series, but Excel charts data according to the following rules:

1.   If the selected range contains more rows than columns of data, Excel plots the data series by columns.

X-axis labels   1st data series   2nd data series   3rd data series

2.   If the selected range contains more columns than rows of data, or the same number of columns and rows, Excel plots the data series by rows.

Legend   X-axis labels   ➤———➤
labels   1st data series   ➤———➤
           2nd data series   ➤———➤

If you select a range to chart which includes column and row headings, and text above or to the left of the numeric data, Excel uses the text to create the axis labels, legends, and title.

If your data selection does not obey these rules, you must tell Excel how your data series is structured in the 2nd Chart Wizard dialogue box.

Editing a Chart:

The easiest way to edit a chart is to right-click it while pointing within the chart area, but near its outer rim. This displays the shortcut menu shown here. As a chart is made up of several objects, for example, data series, plot area, the various axis data area, legends, and chart area, you will get a different shortcut menu if you were pointing to these different areas. Try it. As you right-click different areas, their name will appear in the 'Name box' which is situated below the 'Font' box. The shortcut menu shown here is the one you will get when you right-click the 'Chart Area'.

We have already used the first menu option to format our chart. The second menu option allows you to quickly change the chart type, while the third option can be used to change the source data. The fourth menu option allows you to add Titles, change axes, add grid lines and data labels, while the fifth option lets you specify whether you want your chart to be located in a new sheet or where you created.

Saving Charts:

When you save a workbook, the chart or charts you have created are saved with it. It is, therefore, a good idea not only to give each chart a title, but to also locate it on a differently named sheet.

Use the **Chart Options** in the above shortcut menu to give this chart the title **Yearly Income**, and the **Location** option to put the chart on a separate sheet and give it the name **Income Bar**. Finally, save the workbook under the filename **Project 8**.

Pre-defined Chart Types

To select a different type of chart, click the Chart Wizard icon shown here, or select the **Insert, Chart** command. The 1st Chart Wizard dialogue box displayed previously, lists 14 different chart options. These chart-types are normally used to describe the following relationships between data:

 Area: for showing a volume relationship between two series, such as production or sales, over a given length of time.

Bar: for comparing differences in data (non-continuous data that are not related over time) by depicting changes in horizontal bars to show positive and negative variations from a given position.

 Bubble: for showing a type of XY (scatter) chart. The size of the data (radius of the bubble) indicates the value of a third variable.

Column: for comparing separate items (non-continuous data which are related over time) by depicting changes in vertical bars to show positive and negative variations from a given position.

 Cone: for showing 3-D column and bar charts in a more dramatic way.

Cylinder: similar to Cone.

 Doughnut: for comparing parts with the whole. Similar to pie charts, but can depict more than one series of data.

138

	Line:	for showing continuous changes in data with time.
	Pie:	for comparing parts with the whole. You can use this type of chart when you want to compare the percentage of an item from a single series of data with the whole series.
	Pyramid:	similar to Cone.
	Radar:	for plotting one series of data as angle values defined in radians, against one or more series defined in terms of a radius.
	Surface:	for showing optimum combinations between two sets of data, as in a topographic map. Colours and patterns indicate areas that are in the same range of values.
	Stock:	for showing high-low-close type of data variation to illustrate stock market prices or temperature changes.
	XY:	for showing scatter relationships between X and Y. Scatter charts are used to depict items which are not related over time.

You can change the type of chart by selecting one of the fourteen alternate chart types from the 1st Chart Wizard dialogue box, provided your data fits the selection.

Customising a Chart

In order to customise a chart, you need to know how to add legends, titles, text labels, arrows, and how to change the colour and pattern of the chart background, plot areas and chart markers, and how to select, move and size chart objects.

Drawing a Multiple Column Chart:

As an exercise, we will consider a new column chart which deals with the quarterly 'Costs' of Adept Consultants. To achieve this, first select the Consolidation sheet of workbook **Project 8**, then highlight the cell range A3:E3, press the <Ctrl> key, and while holding it down, use the mouse to select the costs range A6:E11.

Next, click the Chart Wizard icon (or use the **Insert, Chart** command), select Column from the **Chart type** list, click the fourth **Chart sub-type** option, and press the **Next** button. The 6 different quarterly costs will be drawn automatically, as displayed in the composite screen dump below.

Because the selected range contains more rows than columns of data, Excel follows the 1st rule of data series selection which, however, might not be what you want.

To have the 'quarters' appearing on the x-axis and the 'costs' as the legends, we need to tell Excel that our data series is in rows by clicking the **Rows** button on the 2nd Chart Wizard dialogue box. Immediately this is done the column chart changes to:

The chart title and axes titles were inserted by typing the heading 'PROJECT ANALYSIS - Year Summary' in the **Chart title** box of the 3rd Chart Wizard dialogue box, followed by the **Axis Titles** shown above.

Once you are satisfied with your efforts, click the **As new sheet** radio button of the 4th Chart Wizard dialogue box, and name your chart **Costs Bar**. If you make a mistake and you want to try again, make sure the unwanted chart is selected, then press the <Del> key. Finally, save your work under the filename **Project 9**.

Changing a Title and an Axis Label:

To change a title, an axis label, or a legend within a chart, click the appropriate area on the chart. This reveals that these are individual objects (they are surrounded by small black squares) and you can edit, re-position them, or change their font and point size.

You can even rotate text within such areas in any direction you like.

To demonstrate these options, we will use the **Costs Bar** chart saved in **Project 9**, so get it on screen if you are to follow our suggestions.

To change the font size of a chart title, click the Chart Title area to select it and double-click on the border that is displayed when you select such an object. Doing this, displays the Format dialogue box for the selected object, and clicking the Font tab reveals the following:

From here, we changed the font size of the chart title from 10 to 16 points. We also selected the Costs label and changed its size to 14 points, then clicked the Alignment tab to change its orientation to 90°, as shown on the next page.

Drawing a Pie Chart:

To change the chart type, simply select the chart, then click the Chart Wizard and choose the 3-D Pie chart from the displayed list. If the selected chart was the 'quarterly costs' chart, then clicking the **Next** button and pressing the Series tab of the displayed dialogue box, shows the chart type that would be redrawn for the specified data series, as below.

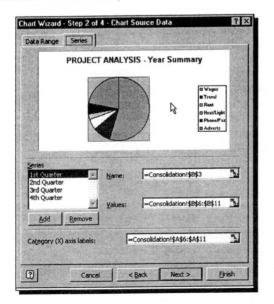

In our case, the pie chart for the 1st Quarter is displayed in the dialogue box. Other quarters could be selected. However, so as not to spoil your **Costs Bar** chart, click the **Cancel** button at this stage.

To obtain a different pie chart, you must select the data range again, then click the Chart Wizard, choose the pie chart from the displayed chart types, then select the specific pie chart that best fits your data, specify the type of series, and give the chart a title.

As a last example in chart drawing, we will use the data range A6:A11 and F6:F11 of the Consolidation worksheet to plot a 3-D pie chart. The steps are the same as before, but for the 3-D option and specifying the type of series data as 'columns'. Note that the chart title should now reflect the Year Totals, rather than the Quarter summaries. The result should be as follows:

To display the above chart, we clicked the Data Labels tab and the **Show label and percent** radio button in the 3rd dialogue box of the Chart Wizard.

This chart tells us, for example, that Wages for the whole year amount to 60% of the total yearly costs. Other cost categories are also displayed with their appropriate percentages. Clicking the **Finish** button displays the pie chart in its finished form, as shown below.

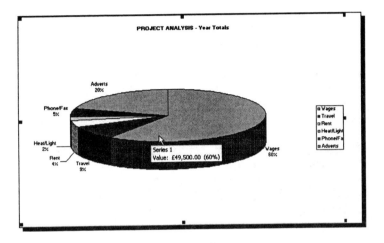

Pointing to any pie slice, causes the pop-up poster to be displayed, informing you of the actual data series, its value and its percentage of the whole. It is now obvious that the information contained in this chart is much more than in the 2-D version.

If you want to explode an individual pie slice, you can do so by simply dragging it. This is possible as each slice is treated as a separate object, but you must increase the size of your chart before you can accurately pinpoint the required slice.

Finally, use the **Chart, Location** menu command to name this last version of the pie chart as **Costs Pie** and save your workbook.

* * *

Excel has many more features than the ones we have introduced in this book. For example, you could use Excel's database and macro capabilities, and also explore its various tools, such as the Goal Seek, Scenarios, Auditing, and Solver. We hope we have given you sufficient basic knowledge to be able to explore these topics by yourself.

However, if you would prefer to be guided through these topics, then may we suggest you look up the later chapters of the book *MS Excel 97 explained* (BP429), also published by BERNARD BABANI (publishing) Ltd.

* * *

9. THE POWERPOINT ENVIRONMENT

Microsoft PowerPoint 97 is a powerful and versatile Graphics Presentation package which, however, is probably the least used of the MS-Office components.

The key element of PowerPoint is the Slide Show and the production of ancillary material, such as scripted notes to accompany each slide, laser copies of slides, and an outline view of all the information in the presentation. However, Microsoft uses the word slide to refer to each individual page of a presentation and you can format the output for overhead projector acetates, or electronic presentation on screen.

In addition, you can apply the skills you have already gained in using Word and Excel and use material created in these applications within PowerPoint.

Starting the PowerPoint Program

PowerPoint is started in Windows either by clicking the **Start** button then selecting **Program** and clicking on the 'Microsoft PowerPoint' icon on the cascade menu, clicking the PowerPoint icon on the Old Office Shortcut Bar, or by clicking the 'Open a Document' icon on the Office Shortcut Bar and double-clicking on a PowerPoint presentation file. In the latter case the presentation will be loaded into PowerPoint at the same time.

The first time you use PowerPoint, it might be a good idea to activate the Assistant and type 'what's new' in the text box, then click **Search**.

This causes the following Help screen to be displayed. Clicking the 'What's new in PowerPoint 97' menu option, opens up a Help dialogue box with the same name, as shown below.

We suggest you spend a little time here browsing through the various help screens. After doing so, click the **Help Topics** button at the top left of the dialogue box to display more information on PowerPoint 97.

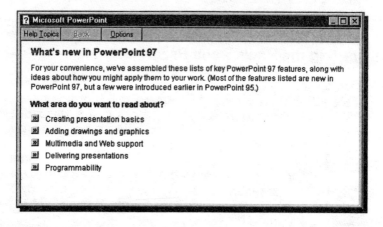

There are even more help topics, including 'Key information' hidden away within the Help System. To reach these topics, click the 'see more' down-arrow button on the Assistant's help screen (the first one on this page), then select the last help topic 'What's New in PowerPoint' from the displayed menu. A similar screen to the second screen dump above opens up, and clicking its **Help Topics** button reveals a wealth of extra information on PowerPoint. Try it!

The PowerPoint Screen

When PowerPoint is loaded, a screen displays with similar Title bar, Menu bar, Toolbar and Formatting bar to those of Word and Excel. Obviously there are differences, but that is to be expected as PowerPoint serves a different purpose to the other programs.

The opening screen of PowerPoint is shown below. The program follows the usual Microsoft Windows conventions with which you should be very familiar by now. Scroll bars and scroll buttons only appear within the window in which you load a presentation.

In the middle of the opening screen, the PowerPoint dialogue box is displayed. The options in this dialogue box make it easy for you to start your presentation.

These options allow you to create a new presentation, as follows:

AutoContent Wizard — Activates a Wizard that helps you determine the content and organisation of your presentation.

Template — Allows you to select a presentation template that determines the colour scheme, fonts, and other design features of the presentation.

Blank Presentation — Allows you to start with a blank presentation with all values for colour scheme, fonts, and other design features set to default values. The same dialogue box also displays when you click the New icon on the Standard Toolbar, shown here.

The last option, at the bottom of the PowerPoint dialogue box, allows you to **Open an Existing Presentation**. Clicking this option, displays the File Open dialogue box which also displays when you click the Open icon on the Standard Toolbar, shown here.

From the File Open dialogue box, you can select where to look for your presentation files, or name a given presentation and let the program find it for you. You can even create a list of favourite presentations. The one shown on the next page is the Progress file which can be found in the **Wizards** folder which itself is in the **Powerpnt** folder. Note the information given on the Status Bar at the bottom of the screen. In this particular case it tells you that you are looking at the first of nine slides using the Multbars Design.

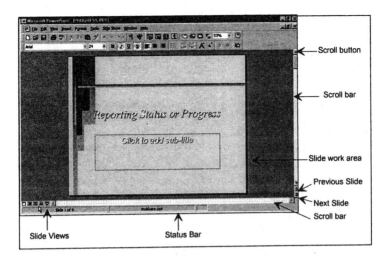

| Scroll button |
| Scroll bar |
| Slide work area |
| Previous Slide |
| Next Slide |
| Scroll bar |

Slide Views   Status Bar

PowerPoint Views

The Slide Views bar at the bottom left corner of the Presentation window, is shown enlarged below.

Slide View   Outline View   Slide Sorter View   Notes Pages View   Slide Show

These five Slide View buttons are the key to the editing power of PowerPoint. They allow you to replace the main Slide View edit window with an Outline View of the text which you can also edit. The Slide Sorter View displays thumbnail views of your work, and the Notes Pages View displays the notes page containing your scripted comments. Finally, the Slide Show view allows you to see your work as an electronic presentation on screen.

Outline View:

In Outline View, your work displays the slide titles and main text in typical outline mode. It is the easiest way of organising and editing presentation text.

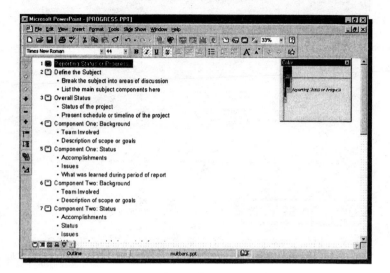

Slide Sorter View:

In this view, you can see the whole presentation at once. You can reorder slides, add transitions, and set timing for electronic presentations.

Notes Pages View:

This is where you create speaker's notes for any or all of your presentation slides.

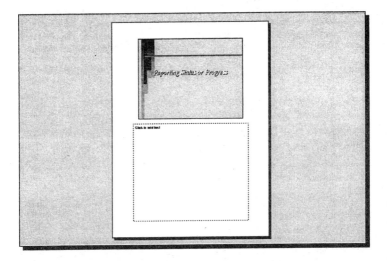

Slide Show View:

In this view you see your work as an electronic presentation, with each slide filling the screen. You can also see the effect of the transitions and timing that you set in the Slide Sorter View.

To see the next slide in full-screen view click the left mouse button. To return to a previous PowerPoint view from a full-screen Slide Show View, press <Esc>, or click the right mouse button to display the quick menu, shown here, and click the **End Show** menu option.

The fourth and fifth menu options can be used in the following way:

While you are showing a slide show, you can take minutes, record action items, and add to your notes pages by right-clicking a slide while in full-view and selecting the **Meeting Minder** menu option which opens the dialogue box shown here.

Such notes only appear on your screen - other participants see only the slide show. Action items appear on a new slide at the end of your slide show and can be posted to Microsoft Outlook, or can be transferred to a new Word document and then printed with that document.

While preparing a presentation, you can make notes relating to each slide by right-clicking a slide while in full-screen view and selecting the **Speaker Notes** menu option. This displays the dialogue box shown here. These notes can be printed and then used either to remember key points during a presentation, or to help the audience follow the

presentation. Both the notes and handout pages have masters, where you can add items you want to appear on each page.

If you have set timings for a slide show using the **Slide Show, Rehearse Timings** command, but want to control the presentation by manually advancing through the slides, you can right-click a slide while in full-screen view and select the **Slide Meter** menu option to measure your progress against the rehearsed times. This opens the dialogue box shown on the next page.

Numbers at the top of the
meter display the elapsed
time for the current slide,
and numbers near the
bottom display the elapsed
time for the slide show.
The progress bar in the

middle measures how you are doing compared with the
rehearsed time. If you are within the rehearsed time,
green boxes appear on the progress bar, while if you go
beyond the rehearsed time, first yellow boxes then red
boxes appear on the progress bar. The bar along the
bottom of the meter indicates whether you are going
too fast or too slow based on your rehearsed timings.

Such control can be achieved while showing a slide
show by clicking the left mouse button to display the
next slide in the show irrespective of the rehearsed
time. Holding down the left button displays the current
slide for a longer time than the rehearsed time. This
feature is useful when you have a set amount of time
for a presentation and want to advance or retard the
ending of the session.

The Slide Master

While a slide is selected, you can get a lot of help from
the Assistant if you do the following:

- Click on the Assistant to open the 'What would
  you like to do?' help box, type the string 'Slide
  Master', as shown below, and click the **Search**
  button.

- In the displayed dialogue box, select the first option 'The slide master' and click the **Search** button.

This opens up an extremely useful help screen, shown below, from which you can learn a lot.

Even though we will be covering in the next chapter most of the points raised in the above help screen, it will be a good idea if you spend some time with it.

10. DESIGNING A PRESENTATION

In this chapter we will use PowerPoint's Wizards to design a simple presentation quickly and effectively. Below, we show the first page of the finished presentation in black and white overhead format, so that you can have an idea of the overall design.

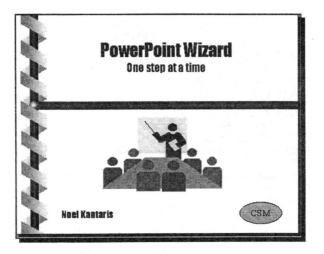

The AutoContent Wizard

When you first start PowerPoint, you are offered the opportunity to use the Wizard, select a template on which to base your work, or begin with a blank presentation.

Most users would, without question, like to produce a presentation in no time at all. The **AutoContent wizard** is an excellent starting point, even if you know what you want to do and how to do it. Therefore, select it in the opening PowerPoint dialogue box, shown on page 149.

Later you can customise your presentation using PowerPoint's editing tools. But for now, clicking the **OK** button, starts the display of six dialogue boxes in which you are:

- Provided with ideas and an organisation for your presentation.

- Asked to select the type of presentation you are going to give (we selected *Generic*).

- Asked to specify how your presentation is going to be used.

- Asked to specify what type of output you require (we selected *Black and white overheads*).

- Asked to type in the title of your presentation (we typed *PowerPoint Wizard*, and deleted the contents of **Additional information**).

- Informed that this is the only information required to create your presentation.

Clicking the **Finish** button, creates your presentation and displays it in Outline mode complete with suggested topics. These can be changed to suite your needs, as shown on the next page.

We have added some extra demoted (more indented) topics using the Demote button on the Outline Toolbar, shown here, and deleted topics that were of no relevance to our presentation.

To return to the original bulleted level from a demoted level, you have to use the Promote button on the Outline Toolbar.

The result of our efforts can be displayed on screen, as shown below, by clicking the Slide View button at the bottom of the screen.

Presentation files that were originally in colour can be toggled between black and white and colour, by simply clicking the Black and White View button shown here.

Save the result of your work so far under the filename **Training 1**.

Clicking the Slide Sorter View button at the bottom of the screen, displays all the slides in your presentation, as follows:

The order of the slides can be changed by simply left-clicking at a slide and dragging the modified pointer to its new position.

Selecting a Template

Our presentation might not look exactly what we had in mind, but we can select a different template to change the overall design. To change the default design of slides, do the following:

- Double-click the area at the bottom of the screen on the Status bar that holds the name of the current template (in our example this should read **Default Design**). This opens the Apply Design dialogue box, and clicking the down-arrow against the **Look in** text box, displays the following:

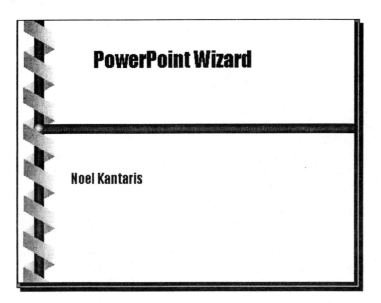

- Double-click the Presentation Design folder which is in the Templates folder, select the **high voltage.pot** design, and click the **Apply** button.

What appears on your screen now is the following display (shown here in black and white format):

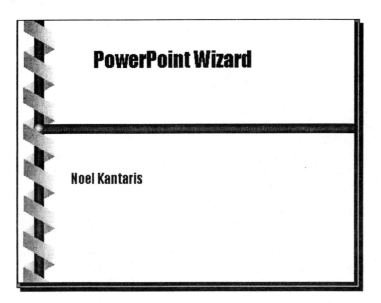

PowerPoint Wizard

Noel Kantaris

Adding a Drawing to a Presentation:

You can use the Office Art tools at the bottom of the screen (if not activated use the **View, Toolbars, Drawing** command) to add to your presentation.

The various buttons on the Office Art toolbar have the following functions (see also next page):

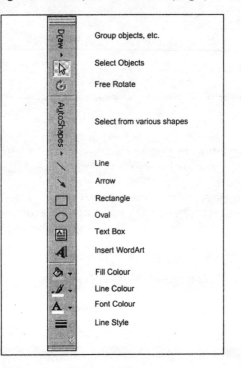

To use these various tools, you must have a Presentation window open. The one shown on the next page is the **high voltage.pot** design.

 We used the Oval tool, the Text Box tool, and the Fill Colour tool to produce the logo shown here, which we placed at the bottom right corner of our presentation. You, of course, can use your drawing skills to produce your own logo. Save your creation under **Training 2**.

Office Art:

Office Art is the new drawing tool shared by all Office 97 applications and gives PowerPoint a superior graphics capability. New or enhanced features are:

AutoShapes – the additional AutoShape categories, such as connectors, block arrows, flowchart symbols, stars and banners, callouts, and action buttons make drawing diagrams much easier.

Bezier curves – used to easily create exact curves with pin-point precision.

3-D effects – allow you to transform 2-D shapes into realistic 3-D objects with new 3-D effects, such as changing the lighting perspective of a 3-D object.

Perspective shadows – allow you to select from a wide range of shadows with perspective, and you can adjust the depth and angle of each shadow to make pictures more realistic.

Connectors – used to create diagrams and flowcharts with new straight, angled, and curved connectors between the shapes; when shapes are moved, the connectors remain attached and automatically reposition themselves.

Arrowhead styles – allow you to change the width and height of arrowheads for maximum effect.

Object alignment – allow you to distribute and space objects evenly, both horizontally and vertically.

Precise line-width control – allows you increased control over the width of lines by selecting preset options or customised line widths.

Image editing – lets you easily adjust the brightness or contrast of a picture.

Transparent background – allows you to insert a bitmap on your slides or Web pages so as to appear to be part of the design by turning background colours into transparent areas.

Rearranging Items in a Presentation:

Items on a presentation slide can be moved to a different position, unless they are part of the template design. For example, the horizontal tube on our design cannot be moved, even though it would be better to have it slightly higher. We could, of course, change the template design by double-clicking its name on the Status bar and selecting a different design.

Below, we show the process of moving the main title from its present position to a new position slightly lower than before, as shown by the dotted rectangles. To achieve this, do the following:

- Point within the text area of the title and when the mouse pointer changes to an insertion bar, click the left mouse button. This causes a border to appear around the title with small handles on it, which can be used to increase or decrease the size of the border.

- To move the title, place the mouse pointer on the title border and when the mouse pointer changes to four small arrows in the shape of a cross, drag the border to its new position.

Inserting a ClipArt Image

To personalise our work, let us insert a clip art image on the front page of our presentation. To do this, click the Insert ClipArt button on the Toolbar, shown here. This opens the Microsoft ClipArt Gallery, provided you have the means of accessing it, from which you can choose a picture.

Usually, the ClipArt Gallery is held on a CD-ROM disc because of its size. Note the different categories; there are 49 in all, each one of which has between 25 to 100 images. We chose the first image of the first row of the Academic category.

Clicking the **Insert** button, transfers the image onto the title page of our presentation.

If you do not have access to the Microsoft ClipArt Gallery, you could always draw your own design. Our final result (we will tell you what text enhancements to apply), is on the next page.

To obtain the design shown below, do the following:

- Move the name of the presentation author to the bottom left corner of the presentation, select the name by clicking on it and reduce the font size to 24. This helps to reduce the prominence of the author's name on the slide, and allows a large enough space to be created in the middle of the slide for the enlargement of the ClipArt object.

- Select the title and click the Text Box tool to allow you to add the words 'One step at a time' below the main title, reduce its font size to 28 and centre it below the title.

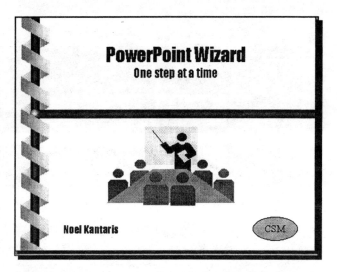

Save the final presentation as **Training 3**. PowerPoint inserts the three letter extension **.ppt**, which however you cannot normally see, to distinguish such files from others in the Office suite.

In the future, double-clicking on this file in a My Computer or Explorer window, will open PowerPoint with the file active.

The Picture Bar:

Note that when you select an inserted picture in a presentation, the Picture Bar is automatically displayed next to the Drawing Bar. The tools on this bar can be used to manipulate pictures to suit your needs. Their functions are as follows:

Insert Picture from File

Image Control

More Contrast

Less Contrast

More Brightness

Less Brightness

Crop

Line Style

Recolor Picture

Format Picture

Set Transparent Color

Reset Picture

Try using these tools on an imported image to see how you can enhance or utterly destroy it! If, at the end of the day, you don't save it, it doesn't matter what you do to it. Just experiment.

As an exercise, try to change the template of our presentation to that of 'Introducing a Speaker' (using the **Format Apply** command), and change the first slide of it to the following:

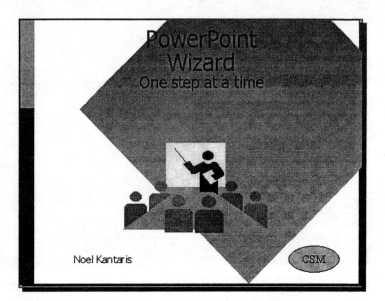

* * *

PowerPoint is obviously capable of a lot more than we have introduced here, but you should now have the confidence to explore more of the package by yourself.

* * *

11. THE ACCESS DATABASE

Microsoft Access is a database management system (DBMS) designed to allow users to store, manipulate and retrieve information easily and quickly. A database is a collection of data that exists and is organised around a specific theme or requirement. It can be of the 'flat-file' type, or it can have relational capabilities, as in the case of Access, which is known as a relational database management system (RDBMS).

The main difference between flat-file and relational database systems is that the latter can store and manipulate data in multiple 'tables', while the former systems can only manipulate a single table at any given time. To make accessing the data easier, each row (or **record**) of data within a database table is structured in the same fashion, i.e., each record will have the same number of columns (or **fields**).

We define a database and its various elements as:

Database	A collection of data organised for a specific theme in one or more tables.
Table	A two-dimensional structure in which data is stored, like in a spreadsheet
Record	A row of information in a table relating to a single entry and comprising one or more fields.
Field	A single column of information of the same type, such as people's names.

In Access 97 the maximum size of a database is 1 gigabyte and can include linked tables in other files. The number of objects in a database is limited to 32,768, while the maximum number of fields in a table is limited to 255.

A good example of a flat-file database is the invoicing details kept on clients by a company. These details could include name of client, description of work done, invoice number, and amount charged, as follows:

NAME	Consultancy	Invoice	Value
VORTEX Co. Ltd	Wind Tunnel Tests	9701	120.84
AVON Construction	Adhesive Tests	9702	103.52
BARROWS Associates	Tunnel Design Tests	9703	99.32
STONEAGE Ltd	Carbon Dating Tests	9704	55.98
PARKWAY Gravel	Material Size Tests	9705	180.22
WESTWOOD Ltd	Load Bearing Tests	9706	68.52

Such a flat-file DBMS is too limited for the type of information normally held by most companies. If the same client asks for work to be carried out regularly, then the details for that client (which could include address, telephone and fax numbers, contact name, date of invoice, etc.), will have to be entered several times. This can lead to errors, but above all to redundant information being kept on a client - each entry will have to have the name of the client, their address, telephone and fax numbers.

The relational facilities offered by Access, overcome the problems of entry errors and duplication of information. The ability to handle multiple tables at any one time allows for the grouping of data into sensible subsets. For example, one table, called client, could hold the names of the clients, their addresses, telephone and fax numbers, while another table, called invoice, could hold information on the work done, invoice number, date of issue, and amount charged. The two tables must have one unique common field, such as a client reference number. The advantage is that details of each client are entered and stored only once, thus reducing the time and effort wasted on entering duplicate information, and also reducing the space required for data storage.

Starting the Access Program

Access is started in Windows either by clicking the **Start** button then selecting **P**rogram and clicking on

the 'Microsoft Access' icon on the cascade menu, clicking the Access icon on the Old Office Shortcut Bar, or by clicking the 'Open a Document' icon on the Office Shortcut Bar

and double-clicking on an Access database file. In the latter case the database will be loaded into Access at the same time.

When you start the Access program by double-clicking its icon, the following dialogue box is displayed on your screen:

From this dialogue box, you can either create a new database, or **O**pen an Existing Database. If you elect to create a new database, then you can select either to create a **B**lank Database, or use the **D**atabase Wizard to help you with the creation of the new database.

Access 97 makes extensive use of Wizards, which have been designed to help the new user to create databases more easily. In particular, the Database Wizard builds the necessary elements for 22 different databases for both home and business use. All you have to do is to answer a set of questions and the Wizard builds the database for you.

Parts of the Access Screen

Before we start designing a database, let us take a look at the Access opening screen. Below we also show the *what's new* help topic displaying its list.

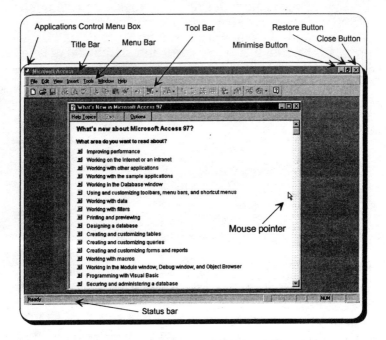

As you can see, these windows have common screen elements with those of other MS Office applications. As usual, depending on what you are doing with Access, the items on the menu bar can be different from those of the opening screen. For example, once a database table is opened the menu bar changes to the following:

Using Help in Access

The first time you start Access, it might be a good idea to look at the help available to you. To do this, cancel the opening dialogue box, then select the **Help, Contents and Index** command which causes the following Help screen to be displayed.

We suggest you spend a little time here browsing through the various help screens, particularly the first three; 'Welcome', 'Introduction', and 'Getting Help'. After doing so, click the Index tab of the Help Topics dialogue box, and type the text *database*. The following screen is then displayed.

Help Topics: Microsoft Access 97

Contents | Index | Find

1 Type the first few letters of the word you're looking for.

Database

2 Click the index entry you want, and then click Display.

> updating
> **Database data type**
> database design
> Database Documenter
> database engine driver
> Database object
> database objects
>   active object
>   backing up
>   copying
>   deleting
>   descriptive text
>   exporting
>   hiding
>   icons in Database window
>   identifier
>   importing and linking

Display   Print...   Cancel

Have a look at the 'database design' topic. On selecting it and clicking the **Display** button, an additional screen opens up, as follows:

Topics Found

Click a topic, then click Display.

> **About designing a database**
> About relationships in a database
> Databases: What they are and how they work
> Designate the Design Master While in Briefcase
> Purpose and features of the Table Analyzer Wizard's query
> Suggestions when changing the design of a replicated database
> View, print, output, or save the design characteristics of database objects
> What is referential integrity?
> What's new with database design?

Display   Cancel

Database Elements

Before we start designing a database using Microsoft Access, it will be a good idea if we looked at the various elements that make up a database. To do so, start Access, which opens the Microsoft Access dialogue box.

Next, and if this is being done immediately after starting Access, select the **Database Wizard** option and click **OK**. Otherwise, either click the New Database icon, shown to the left, or use the **File, New Database** command. Any one of these three methods will cause the New Database dialogue box to be displayed, as shown below, provided the General tab is the active dialogue box tab at the time.

To create a new database, press the **OK** button. This opens the File New Database dialogue box shown on the next page.

In the **File name** box, type the database name, say
Adept 1, which replaces the default name **db1**. Access
adds the extension **.mdb** which, however, you don't
normally see. We also decided to save this example on
floppy disc, therefore we clicked the down arrow
against the **Save in** box and selected the 3½" **Floppy
(A:)** drive. Finally, pressing the **Create** button displays
the Database dialogue box as follows:

It is from here that you can design the various
elements that make up a database, such as Tables,
Queries, Forms, and Reports, all of which we will
examine in some detail in this and the next three
chapters.

Creating a Table

To design a database table, select the Tables tab and click the **New** button on the Database dialogue box, which displays the New Table, shown below immediately below the Database window. The first two options on the list, allow you to start designing a table from scratch, while the third option allows you to automatically select from a list of pre-defined table applications. The penultimate option allows you to import tables and objects from an external file into the current database, while the last option allows you to link a table in the current database to external tables.

Selecting the third option and pressing **OK**, opens the Table Wizard dialogue box, shown at the lower right corner of the composite screen dump above.

The database we are going to create holds the invoicing details which the firm Adept Consultants keep on their clients. One table will hold the details of the clients, while another will hold the actual invoice details.

179

Choose 'Customers' from the **Sample Tables** list of the Table Wizard dialogue box, to reveal a list of appropriate fields for that table.

You can either select all the fields or you can select a few. For our example, we selected the following fields: CustomerID, CompanyName, BillingAddress, City, StateOrProvince, PostalCode, ContactTitle, PhoneNumber, FaxNumber and Notes, by highlighting each in turn and pressing the ▣ button.

Don't worry if these field names are not exactly what you want, as they can be easily changed. To change field names, highlight them in turn in the 'Fields in my

new table' list and click the **Rename Field** button to reveal the Rename field dialogue box shown here.

We suggest you change the selected field names to those listed below.

CustomerID	CustomerID
CompanyName	Name
BillingAddress	Address
City	Town
StateOrProvince	County
PostalCode	PostCode
ContactTitle	Contact
PhoneNumber	Phone
FaxNumber	Fax
Notes	Order

When you have completed renaming the field names, press the **Finish** button, which displays the Customers Table ready for you to enter information.

To redesign the table, including changing its field names, click the Design View icon shown here, or use the **View, Table Design** command. The following Table is displayed.

As each field name is highlighted, a Field Properties box appears at the bottom of the screen. If you were using this Table View to rename fields, then you should also edit the name appearing against the Caption property, or remove it altogether.

Next, place the cursor at the end of the Data Type descriptor of the CustomerID field which causes a down-arrow button to be displayed. Clicking this button, displays a drop-down list of data types, as shown here.

As we intend to use the first four letters of a company's name as the CustomerID field, change the current data type from Counter to Text. Similarly, change the data type of the last field (Order) from Memo to AutoNumber. Finally, place the cursor against the Phone and Fax fields and delete the entry against the Input Mask in the Field Properties box. The type of input mask displayed here is ideal for USA Phone and Fax numbers, but it does not correspond to the entry form usually adopted in the UK, so it is best removed.

Finally, first click the Save icon (or use the **File, Save** command) to save your design changes, then click the Datasheet View icon (or use the **View, Datasheet** command) to revert to the Customers table so that you can start entering information, as shown below.

Customer ID	Name	Address	Town	County	Post Code	Contact
VORT	VORTEX Co. Ltd	Windy House	St. Austell	Cornwall	TR18 1FX	Brian Storm
AVON	AVON Construction	Riverside House	Stratford-on-Avon	Warwickshire	AV15 2QW	John Waters
BARR	BARROWS Associates	Barrows House	Bodmin	Cornwall	PL22 1XE	Mandy Brown
STON	STONEAGE Ltd	Data House	Salisbury	Wiltshire	SB44 1BN	Mike Irons
PARK	PARKWAY Gravel	Aggregate House	Bristol	Avon	BS55 2ZX	James Stone
WEST	WESTWOOD Ltd	Weight House	Plymouth	Devon	PL22 1AA	Mary Slim
GLOW	GLOWORM Ltd	Light House	Brighton	Sussex	BR87 4DD	Peter Summers
SILV	SILVERSMITH Co	Radiation House	Exeter	Devon	EX28 1PL	Adam Smith
WORM	WORMGLAZE Ltd	Glass House	Winchester	Hampshire	WN23 5TR	Richard Glazer
EALI	EALING Engines Design	Engine House	Taunton	Somerset	TN17 3RT	Trevor Miles
HIRE	HIRE Service Equipment	Network House	Bath	Avon	BA76 3WE	Nicole Webb
EURO	EUROBASE Co. Ltd	Control House	Penzance	Cornwall	TR15 8LK	Sarah Star

The widths of the above fields were changed so that all fields could be visible on the screen at the same time.

To change the width of a field, place the cursor on the column separator until the cursor changes to the vertical split arrow, then drag the column separator to the right or left, to increase or decrease the width of the field.

Sorting a Database Table:

As you enter information into a database table, you might elect to change the field headings by clicking the Design Table icon and editing a field name, say from Name to CompanyName. If you do this, on return to the Customers table you will find that the records have sorted automatically in ascending order of the entries of the field in which you left the cursor while in the Design Table.

Contact	Phone	Fax	Order
Brian Storm	01776-223344	01776-224466	1
John Waters	01657-113355	01657-221133	2
Mandy Brown	01554-664422	01554-663311	3
Mike Irons	01765-234567	01765-232332	4
James Stone	01534-987654	01534-984567	5
Mary Slim	01234-667755	01234-669988	6
Peter Summers	01432-746523	01432-742266	7
Adam Smith	01336-997755	01336-996644	8
Richard Glazer	01123-654321	01123-651234	9
Trevor Miles	01336-010107	01336-010109	10
Nicole Webb	01875-558822	01875-552288	11
Sarah Star	01736-098765	01736-098567	12
			(AutoNumber)

If you want to preserve the order in which you entered your data, then sort by the last field (Order) with its type as AutoNumber. This can be done at any time, even after you finished entering all other information in your table.

Sorting a database table in ascending order of an AutoNumber type field, results in the database table displaying in the order in which the data was originally entered in that table. Above, we show the Contact field, so that you can cross-check the original order of your Customer table, as well as the rest of the information in that table not shown in the screen dump of the previous page.

To sort a database table in ascending or descending order of the entries of any field, place the cursor in the required field and click the Sort Ascending or Sort Descending icon, shown here.

With the keyboard, select the **Records, <u>S</u>ort** command, then choose either the **Sort <u>A</u>scending** or the **Sort <u>D</u>escending** option.

Applying a Filter to a Sort:

If you would like to sort and display only records that fit selected criteria, use the **Records, Filter, Advanced Filter/Sort** command, which opens the Filter dialogue box, shown below.

Custom	Name	Address	Town	County	Post Code	Cont:
WEST	WESTWOOD Ltd	Weight House	Plymouth	Devon	PL22 1AA	Mary Sli
WORM	WORMGLAZE Ltd	Glass House	Winchester	Hampshire	WN23 5TR	Richard

Customers
*
CustomerID
Name
Address
Town

Field:	CustomerID				
Sort:	Ascending				
Criteria:	Like "W*"				
or:					

The upper portion of the dialogue box displays all the fields in the Customers table, while the lower portion is where you enter your filter restrictions. In the above example, we chose to view, in ascending order, the records within the CustomersID field that start with W - we typed W* and Access displayed *Like "W*"*.

On pressing the Apply Filter icon, the Customers table displays with only two entries, as seen in the above composite screen dump. To revert to the display of all the records, click the same icon again, which now appears on the Toolbar depressed, and bears the name Remove Filter.

184

Using a Database Form

Once a table has been selected from the Database window, clicking the down-arrow against the New Object button and selecting **AutoForm**, automatically displays each record of that table in form view. The created form for the Customers table is shown below.

Forms can be used to enter, change or view data. They are mainly used to improve the way in which data is displayed on the screen.

Forms can also be used to sort records in a database table in descending or ascending order of a selected field.

When you attempt to close a new **Form** window, you will be asked if you would like to save it. An Access database can have lots of different forms, each designed with a different purpose in mind. Saved forms are displayed in the Database window when you click the Forms tab. In the above example, we chose the default name suggested by Access, which was Customers.

In a later chapter we will discuss Form design in some detail, including their customisation.

Working with Data

Adding Records in a Table: Whether you are in Table view or Form view, to add a record, click the New Record icon, shown here.

When in Table view, the cursor jumps to the first empty record in the table (the one with the asterisk in the box to the left of the first field). When in Form view, Access displays an empty form which can be used to add a new record.

Finding Records in a Table: Whether you are in Table or Form view, to find a record click the Find icon, or use **Edit, Find**. This opens the following dialogue box:

Custon	Name	Address	Town	County	Post Code	Contact
AVON	AVON Construction	Riverside House	Stratford-on-Avc	Warwickshire	AV15 2QW	John Waters
BARR	BARROWS Associat	Barrows House	Bodmin	Cornwall	PL22 1XE	Mandy Brow
EALI	EALING Engines Des	Engine House	Taunton	Somerset	TN17 3RT	Trevor Miles
EURO	EUROBASE Co. Ltd	Control House	Penzance	Cornwall	TR15 8LK	Sarah Star
GLOW	GLOWORM Ltd	Light House	Brighton	Sussex	BR87 4DD	Peter Summ

Find in field: 'Customer ID'

Find What: w*

Search: All

Match: Whole Field

☐ Match Case
☐ Search Fields As Formatted
☑ Search Only Current Field

Find First
Find Next
Close

Note the field name on the Title bar, which is CustomerID, indicating that the cursor was in the CustomerID field before we clicked the Find icon or selected the **Find** command.

To find all the records starting with **w**, we type **w*** in the **Fin̲d What** box of the dialogue box. If the **Search Only Curre̲nt Field** box is ticked, the search is carried out in that field. Pressing the **Find First̲** button, highlights the first record with the CustomerID 'WEST'. Pressing the **F̲ind Next** button, highlights the next record that matches our selected criteria.

Deleting Records from a Table: To delete a record when in Table view, point to the box to the left of the record to highlight the entire record, as shown below, then press the <Del> key.

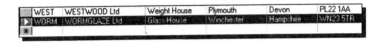

To delete a record when in Form view, first display the record you want to delete, then use the **Edit, Select Record** command to select the whole record, and press the <Del> key.

In both cases you will be given a warning and you will be asked to confirm your decision.

Delete, Insert, and Move Fields in a Table: To delete

a field from a table, close any forms that might be open, then load the table from the Database window, then press the Design View icon, click the row selector to highlight the field you want to remove, as shown below, and press the Delete Row icon, shown here, or use the **Edit, Delete Rows** command.

Field Name	Data Type	
CustomerID	Text	
Name	Text	
Address	Text	
Town	Text	
County	Text	

Customers : Table

To insert a field in a table, display the table in Design

View, and highlight the field above which you want to insert the new field, and press the Insert Row icon, shown here, or use the **Insert, Rows** command.

187

To move a field from its current to a new position in a table, select the field you want to move, then point to the row selector so that the mouse pointer is inclined as shown below, and drag the row to its new position.

Field Name	Data Type
CustomerID	Text
Name	Text
Address	Text
Town	Text
County	Text
Post Code	Text
Contact	Text
Phone	Text
Fax	Text

Note that while you are dragging the field, the mouse pointer changes to the one pointing at the Name field in the above composite. Releasing the mouse button, moves the Contact field to where the Name field is now and pushes all other fields one row down.

Printing a Table View:

You can print a database table by clicking the Print icon, or by using the **File, Print** command to display the Print dialogue box shown below. Alternatively, you can preview a database on screen by clicking the Preview icon.

However, printing directly from here, produces a pre-defined print-out, the format of which you cannot control, apart from the margins and print orientation. To control these, click the **Setup** or **Properties** button.

For a better method of producing a printed output, see the Report Design section.

12. RELATIONAL DATABASE DESIGN

In order to be able to discuss relational databases, we will add to the database of the previous chapter an Orders table. To do this go through the following steps.

- Open the **Adept 1** database and use the **New** button on the Database window to add an Orders table to it.

- Use the Table Wizard and select Orders from the displayed **Sample Tables** list. Next, select the five fields displayed below under **Fields in my new table** from the **Sample Fields** list, and press the **Next** button.

This displays the top dialogue box on the next page, in which you can, if you want to, change the name of the table. We elected to accept the default name, but we clicked the 'No, I'll set the primary key' radio button before pressing the **Next** key.

- On the next dialogue box you can select which field will hold data that is unique for each record. The key field must be unique in a table, and the OrderID field satisfies this requirement. This field is used by Access for fast searches.

- Click the **Numbers and/or letters I enter when I add new records** radio button, before you press the **Next** button.

190

On the next dialogue box you specify whether the new table is related to any other tables in the database. The default is that it is not related.

- Accept the default option, and press the **Next** button to reveal the final dialogue box.

- Select the second option and press the **Finish** button, to let the Wizard create your table.

Although the two tables are actually related, we chose at this stage to tell the Wizard that they are not. This might appear to you as odd, but the Wizard makes certain assumptions about unique fields (for example, that ID fields are numbers), which is not what we want them to be. We choose to remain in control of the design of our database and, therefore, we will define the relationship between the two tables later.

The Wizard displays the newly created table ready for you to enter your data. However, before doing so, use the Design Table facility, as discussed previously, to change the Data Types of the selected Field Names to those displayed below.

Field Name	Data Type	
OrderID	Text	
CustomerID	Text	
EmployeeID	Text	
OrderDate	Date/Time	
ShipDate	Date/Time	

Orders : Table

The information you need to enter in the Orders table is shown below.

Orders : Table

Order ID	Customer ID	Employee ID	Order Date	Ship Date
97085VOR	VORT	A.D. Smith	20/03/97	10/04/97
97097AVO	AVON	W.A. Brown	25/03/97	14/04/97
97099BAR	BARR	S.F. Adams	01/04/97	02/05/97
97002STO	STON	C.H. Wills	20/04/97	25/05/97
97006PAR	PARK	A.D. Smith	13/05/97	16/06/97
97010WES	WEST	W.A. Brown	15/05/97	26/06/97
97018GLO	GLOW	L.S. Stevens	25/06/97	19/07/97
97025SIL	SILV	S.F. Adams	28/06/97	22/07/97
97029WOR	WORM	C.H. Wills	20/07/97	13/08/97
97039EAL	EALI	A.D. Smith	30/07/97	25/08/97
97045HIR	HIRE	W.A. Brown	18/08/97	08/09/97
97051EUR	EURO	L.S. Stevens	25/08/97	19/09/97
97064AVO	AVON	S.F. Adams	20/09/97	15/10/97

Record: 13 ▶ ▶I ▶* of 13

Relationships

Information held in two or more tables of a database is normally related in some way. In our case, the two tables, Customers and Orders, are related by the CustomerID field.

To build up relationships between tables, return to the Database window and press the Relationships icon on the Tool bar, shown here. This opens the following window in which the index field in each table is emboldened.

You can build relationships between tables by dragging a field name from one table into another. In our example below, we have dragged CustomerID from the Customers table (by pointing to it, pressing the left

mouse button, and while keeping the mouse button pressed, dragging the pointer) to the required field in the other table, in this case CustomerID in the Orders table. Releasing the mouse button opens the dialogue boxes shown at the top of the next page (the second one by pressing the **Join Type** button on the first one).

In the Join Properties dialogue box you can specify the type of join Access should create in new queries - more about this later. For the present, press the **OK** button on the Join Properties dialogue box, to close it, then check the **Enforce Referential Integrity** box in the Relationships dialogue box, and press the **Create** button.

Access creates and displays graphically the chosen type of relationship in the Relationships window shown here. Note the relationship '1 customer to many (∞) orders' symbolism in the Relationships window.

Because Access is a relational database, data can be used in queries from more than one table at a time. As we have seen, if the database contains tables with related data, the relationships can be defined easily.

Usually, the matching fields have the same name, as in our example of Customers and Orders tables. In the Customers table, the Customerid field is the primary field and relates to the Customerid field in the Orders table - there can be several orders in the Orders table from one customer in the Customers table.

The various types of relationships are as follows:

- Inherited - for attaching tables from another Access database. The original relationships of the attached database can be used in the current database.

- Referential - for enforcing relationships between records according to certain rules, when you add or delete records in related tables belonging to the same database. For example, you can only add records to a related table, if a matching record already exists in the primary table, and you cannot delete a record from the primary table if matching records exist in a related table.

Viewing and Editing Relationships:

To view the current relationships between tables, activate the Database window and press the Relationships icon. This displays the following:

To edit a relationship, double-click the left mouse button at the pointer position shown on the previous screen dump. The tip of the mouse pointer must be on the inclined line joining the two tables in the Relationships window, as shown, before Access will respond. If you have difficulty with this action, first point to the relationship line and click once to embolden it, then use the **Relationships, Edit Relationship** command. Either of these two actions will open the Relationships dialogue box in which you can change the various options already discussed.

A given relationship can easily be removed altogether, by first activating it (pointing and clicking to embolden it), then pressing the <Del> key. A confirmation dialogue box will be displayed. To delete a table, you must first detach it from other tables, then select it in the Database Window and press the <Del> key. Think before you do this!

Creating an Additional Table

As an exercise, create a third table using the **Table Wizards** and select Invoices from the displayed **Sample Tables** list. Next, select the five fields displayed below - the names and their data types have been changed using the Design Table facility.

Field Name	Data Type
🔑 InvoiceID	Text
CustomerID	Text
Date	Date/Time
Amount	Currency
▶ Paid?	Yes/No

Invoices : Table

Next, enter the data given below and build up appropriate relationships between the Invoices table, the Customers table and the Orders table, as shown on the next page.

AD9701	VORT	10/04/97	£120.84	No
AD9702	AVON	14/04/97	£103.52	Yes
AD9703	BARR	02/05/97	£99.32	No
AD9704	STON	25/05/97	£55.98	No
AD9705	PARK	16/06/97	£180.22	No
AD9706	WEST	26/06/97	£68.52	No
AD9707	GLOW	19/07/97	£111.56	No
AD9708	SILV	22/07/97	£123.45	Yes
AD9709	WORM	13/08/97	£35.87	No
AD9710	EALI	25/08/97	£58.95	No
AD9711	HIRE	08/09/97	£290.00	No
AD9712	EURO	19/09/97	£150.00	No
AD9713	AVON	15/10/97	£135.00	No
				No

The relationships between the three tables should be arranged as follows:

It is important that you should complete this exercise, as it consolidates what we have done so far and, in any case, we will be using all three tables in what comes next. So go ahead and try it.

13. CREATING A QUERY

You create a query so that you can ask questions about the data in your database tables. For example, we could find out whether we have more than one order from the same customer in our Adept database.

To do this, start Access, load **Adept 1**, and in the Database window click the Queries tab, followed by the **New** button which opens the New Query dialogue box. Selecting the **Find Duplicates Query Wizard**, displays the following:

On clicking **OK**, the Find Duplicates Query Wizard dialogue box is displayed, as shown below.

Next, select the Orders table from the displayed database tables in this dialogue box, and press the **Next** button.

On the following dialogue box select **CustomerID** as the field you want to check for duplicate values, then press the 🔲 button, followed by the **Next** button.

Finally, select the additional fields you would like to see along with the duplicate values, by selecting those you want from the next dialogue box, either one at a time or, if you decide to select all of them, as shown here, by clicking the 🔲 button. Clicking the **Finish** button displays the Select Query screen shown below.

Find duplicates for Orders : Select Query				
Customer ID	**Order ID**	**Employee ID**	**Order Date**	**Ship Date**
AVON	97097AVO	W.A. Brown	25/03/97	14/04/97
AVON	97064AVO	S.F. Adams	20/09/97	15/10/97

Record: 1 of 2

If you examine the original Orders table, you will indeed find that it contains two orders from AVON.

Types of Queries

The query we have created so far, is known as the *Select Query*, which is the most common type of query. However, with Access you can also create and use other types of queries, as follows:

- **Crosstab query** - used to present data with row and column headings, just like a spreadsheet. It can be used to summarise large amounts of data in a more readable form.

- **Action query** - used to make changes to many records in one operation. For example, you might like to remove from a given table all records that meet certain criteria, make a new table, or append records to a table. Obviously, this type of query has to be treated with care!

- **Union query** - used to match fields from two or more tables.

- **Pass-through query** - used to pass commands to an SQL (see below) database.

- **Data-definition query** - used to create, change, or delete tables in an Access database using SQL statements.

SQL stands for Structured Query Language, often used to query, update, and manage relational databases. Each query created by Access has an associated SQL statement that defines the action of that query. Thus, if you are familiar with SQL, you can use such statements to view and modify queries, or set form and report properties. However, these actions can be done more easily with the QBE (query-by-example) grid, to be discussed next. If you design union queries, pass-through queries, or data-definition queries, then you must use SQL statements, as these types of queries can not be designed with the QBE grid. Finally, to create a sub-query, you use the QBE grid, but you enter an SQL SELECT statement for criteria, as we shall see in the next QBE grid example.

The Query Window

The Query window is a graphical query-by-example (QBE) tool. Because of Access' graphical features, you can use the mouse to select, drag, and manipulate objects in the query window to define how you would like to see your data.

An example of a ready made Query window can be seen by selecting the Find duplicates for Orders query and clicking the **Design** button on the Database window. This action opens the Select Query dialogue box shown below.

You can add a table to the top half of the Query window by simply dragging the table from the Database window. Similarly, you can add fields to the bottom half of the Query window (the QBE grid) by dragging fields from the tables on the top half of the Query window. In addition, the QBE grid is used to select the sort order of the data, or insert criteria, such as SQL statements.

To see the full SQL SELECT statement written by Access as the criteria selection when we first defined the query, use the **View, SQL View** command.

Note the part of the statement which states 'As Tmp GROUP'. Access collects the data you want as a temporary group, called a *dynaset*. This special set of data behaves like a table, but it is not a table; it is a dynamic view of the data from one or more tables, selected and sorted by the particular query.

Creating a New Query:

Below, we show a screen dump created by first clicking the Queries tab, then pressing the **New** button on the Database window. In the displayed New Query dialogue box, select Design View and press the **OK** button. This opens both the Select Query and the Show Table dialogue boxes shown overleaf.

The Invoices and Customers tables were then added to the Select Query window, as shown below.

Adding Fields to a Query Window:

Below we show a screen in which the Paid? and InvoiceID fields have been dragged from the Invoices table and added to the Query window. In addition, the Name and Contact fields have been dragged from the Customers table and placed on the Query window, while the Phone field from the Customers table is about to be added to the Query window.

Having dragged all five fields from the two tables onto the QBE grid, we have added the word No as the criteria on the Paid? field and selected Ascending as the Sort for the InvoiceID field.

Note that the Invoices and Customers tables are joined by a line that connects the two CustomerID fields. The join line was created when we designed the tables and their relationships in the previous chapter. Even if you have not created these relationships, Access will join the tables in a query automatically when the tables are added to a query, provided each table has a field with the same name and a compatible data type and one of those fields is a primary key. A primary field is displayed in bold in the Query window.

If you have not created relationships between your tables yourself, or Access has not joined your tables automatically, you can still use related data in your query by joining the tables in the Query window.

Clicking the Run icon on the Toolbar, shown here, instantly displays all the unpaid invoices with the details you have asked for, as follows:

Paid?	Order ID	Amount	Invoice No	Name	Contact	Phone
No	97085VOR	£120.84	AD9701	VORTEX Co. Ltd	Brian Storm	01776-223344
No	97099BAR	£99.32	AD9703	BARROWS Associat	Mandy Brown	01554-664422
No	97002STO	£55.98	AD9704	STONEAGE Ltd	Mike Irons	01765-234567
No	97006PAR	£180.22	AD9705	PARKWAY Gravel	James Stone	01534-987654
No	97010WES	£68.52	AD9706	WESTWOOD Ltd	Mary Slim	01234-667755
No	97018GLO	£111.56	AD9707	GLOWORM Ltd	Peter Summe	01432-746523
No	97029WOR	£35.87	AD9709	WORMGLAZE Ltd	Richard Glaze	01123-654321
No	97039EAL	£58.95	AD9710	EALING Engines Des	Trevor Miles	01336-010107
No	97045HIR	£290.00	AD9711	HIRE Service Equipm	Nicole Webb	01875-558822
No	97051EUR	£150.00	AD9712	EUROBASE Co. Ltd	Sarah Star	01736-098765
No	97097AVO	£135.00	AD9713	AVON Construction	John Waters	01657-113355
No	97064AVO	£135.00	AD9713	AVON Construction	John Waters	01657-113355

Unpaid Invoices : Select Query

Record: 1 of 12

To save your newly created query, use the **File, Save As/Export** command, and give it a name such as 'Unpaid Invoices' in the Save As dialogue box.

Types of Criteria

Access accepts the following expressions as criteria:

Arithmetic Operators		Comparison Operators		Logical Operators	
*	Multiply	<	Less than	And	And
/	Divide	<=	Less than or equal	Or	Inclusive or
+	Add	>	Greater than	Xor	Exclusive or
-	Subtract	>=	Greater than or equal	Not	Not equivalent
		=	Equal	Eqv	Equivalent
		<>	Not equal	Imp	Implication

Other operators		
Between	Between 50 And 150	All values between 50 and 150
In	In("Bath","Bristol")	All records with Bath and Bristol
Is	Is Null	All records with no value in that field
Like	Like "Brian *"	All records with Brian something in field
&	[Name]&" "&[Surname]	Concatenates strings

Using Wildcard Characters in Criteria:

In the previous example we used the criteria A* to mean any company whose name starts with the letter A. The asterisk in this criteria is known as a wildcard character.

To search for a pattern, you can use the asterisk (*) and the question mark (?) as wildcard characters when specifying criteria in expressions. An asterisk stands for any number of characters, while a question mark stands for any single character in the same position as the question mark.

The following examples show the use of wildcard characters in various types of expressions:

Entered Expression	Meaning	Examples
a?	Any two-letter word beginning with A	am, an, as, at
???d	Any four-letter word ending with d	find, hand, land yard
Sm?th	Any five-letter word beginning with Sm and ending with th	Smith Smyth
fie*	Any word starting with the letters fie	field, fiend, fierce, fiery
*ght	Any word ending with ght	alight, eight, fight, light, might, sight
*/5/97	All dates in May '97	1/5/97
a	Any word with the letter a in it	Brian, Mary, star, yard

Combining Criteria

By specifying additional criteria in a Query window you can create powerful queries for viewing your data. In the examples below we have added the field Amount to our Unpaid Invoices query.

The AND Criteria with Different Fields: When you insert criteria in several fields, but in the same row, Access assumes that you are searching for records that meet all of the criteria. For example, the criteria below list the records shown on the next page.

Field:	Paid?	Amount	InvoiceID	Name	Contact
Table:	Invoices	Invoices	Invoices	Customers	Customers
Sort:					
Show:	☑	☑	☑	☑	☑
Criteria:	No	Between 50 And 150			Like "M*"
or:					

Paid?	Order ID	Amount	Invoice No	Name	Contact
No	97099BAR	£99.32	AD9703	BARROWS Associates	Mandy Brown
No	97002STO	£55.98	AD9704	STONEAGE Ltd	Mike Irons
No	97010WES	£68.52	AD9706	WESTWOOD Ltd	Mary Slim

Record: 1 of 3

The OR Criteria with the Same Field: If you include multiple criteria in one field only, then Access assumes that you are searching for records that meet any one of the specified criteria. For example, the criteria <50 or >100 in the field Amount, shown below, list the required records, only if the No in the Paid? field is inserted in both rows.

Field:	Paid?	Amount	InvoiceID	Name	Contact
Table:	Invoices	Invoices	Invoices	Customers	Customers
Sort:					
Show:	✓	✓	✓	✓	✓
Criteria:	No	<50			
or:	No	>100			

Paid?	Order ID	Amount	Invoice No	Name	Contact
No	97085VOR	£120.84	AD9701	VORTEX Co. Ltd	Brian Storm
No	97006PAR	£180.22	AD9705	PARKWAY Gravel	James Stone
No	97018GLO	£111.56	AD9707	GLOWORM Ltd	Peter Summe
No	97045HIR	£290.00	AD9711	HIRE Service Equipment	Nicole Webb
No	97051EUR	£150.00	AD9712	EUROBASE Co. Ltd	Sarah Star
No	97097AVO	£135.00	AD9713	AVON Construction	John Waters
No	97064AVO	£135.00	AD9713	AVON Construction	John Waters

Record: 1 of 7

The OR Criteria with Different Fields: If you include multiple criteria in different fields, but in different rows, then Access assumes that you are searching for records that meet either one or the other of the specified criteria. For example, the criteria Yes in the Paid? field and the criteria <50 in the Amount field, but in different rows, list the following records.

Field:	Paid?	Amount	InvoiceID	Name	Contact
Table:	Invoices	Invoices	Invoices	Customers	Customers
Sort:					
Show:	☑	☑	☑	☑	☑
Criteria:	Yes				
or:		<50			

	Paid?	Order ID	Amount	Invoice No	Name	Contact
►	Yes	97097AVO	£103.52	AD9702	AVON Construction	John Waters
	Yes	97064AVO	£103.52	AD9702	AVON Construction	John Waters
	Yes	97025SIL	£123.45	AD9708	SILVERSMITH Co	Adam Smith
	No	97029WOR	£35.87	AD9709	WORMGLAZE Ltd	Richard Glaze

Record: |◄| |◄| | 1 | |►| |►I| |►*| of 4

Unpaid Invoices : Select Query

The AND and OR Criteria Together: The following choice of criteria will cause Access to retrieve either records that have Yes in the Paid? field and the company's name starts with the letter A, or records that the invoice amount is less than £50.

Field:	Paid?	Amount	InvoiceID	Name	Contact
Table:	Invoices	Invoices	Invoices	Customers	Customers
Sort:					
Show:	☑	☑	☑	☑	☑
Criteria:	Yes			Like "A*"	
or:		<50			

209

The retrieved records from such a query are shown below.

	Paid?	Order ID	Amount	Invoice No	Name	Contact
▶	Yes	97097AVO	£103.52	AD9702	AVON Construction	John Waters
	No	97029WOR	£35.87	AD9709	WORMGLAZE Ltd	Richard Glaze

Record: ◀ ◀ [1] ▶ ▶I ▶* of 2   ◀ ▶

Unpaid Invoices : Select Query

Calculating Totals in Queries:

Access allows you to perform calculations on groups of records. For example, to find the total value of unpaid invoices grouped by month, use the following query.

Functions, such as 'sum', are entered in the Total row of a query which can be displayed by clicking the Totals button, shown here, while in Design View. Note the form of the entry in the third column of the Field row. Save this query under the the name 'Monthly invoices'.

Field:	Paid?	Amount	Month: DatePart("m",[Date])
Table:	Invoices	Invoices	
Total:	Group By	Sum	Group By
Sort:			
Show:	☑	☑	☑
Criteria:	No		
or:			

Query1 : Select Query

	Paid?	SumOfAmoun	Month
▶	No	£120.84	4
	No	£155.30	5
	No	£248.74	6
	No	£111.56	7
	No	£94.82	8
	No	£440.00	9
	No	£135.00	10

Record: ◀ ◀ [1] ▶ ▶I ▶* of 7

14. USING FORMS & REPORTS

We saw towards the end of Chapter 11 how easy it was to create a single column form to view our Customers table. To see this again, open **Adept 1** and in the Database window click the Form tab, then double-click on Form1, which should display the following:

You can use forms to find, edit, and add data in a convenient manner. Access provides you with an easy way of designing various types of forms, some of which are discussed here. Forms look good on screen, but do not produce very good output on paper, whereas reports are designed to look good on paper, but do not necessarily look good on screen.

Using the Form Wizard

Using the Form Wizard, you can easily display data from either a table or a query in form view.

In the Database window, first click the Forms tab, then the **New** button which opens the New Form dialogue box in which you must choose either a table or a query on which to base the new form. In the screen dump below, we have chosen the Invoices table.

Next, select the **Chart Wizard** option which causes the Form Wizard to display a number of dialogue boxes. As usual, after making appropriate selections, click the **Next** button to progress through the automatic design of the particular form. As you can see from the above screen dump, there are 7 different types of forms available for you to choose from. Their function will be discussed shortly.

To continue with our example, the Wizard displays the following dialogue box in which you are asked to specify the fields that contain the data you want to chart. We chose InvoiceID and Amount.

This opens another dialogue box in which you are asked what type of chart you would like. We chose the first one on the second row before pressing **Next**.

In the following dialogue box, double-click the x-axis button (the one with the caption 'SumOfAmount') and select 'None' from the list in the displayed Summarize dialogue box, shown below, and press **OK**.

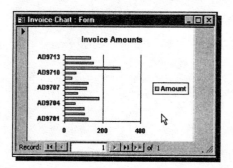

The Wizard then asks you what title and name to give to this form - we chose 'Invoice Amounts' and 'Invoice Chart'.

Pressing the **Finish** button, allows the Wizard to display the final result, shown here to the left. It is as easy as that to get a graphical view of the amounts involved in each of your invoices.

The available choice of Form Wizards have the following function:

Type of Form	Function
Design View	Design a form from scratch.
Form Wizard	Automatically creates a form based on the fields you select.
AutoForm: Columnar	Creates a columnar form with all the field labels appearing in the first column and the data in the second. The form displays one record at a time.
AutoForm: Tabular	Tabulates a screen full of records in tabular form with the field labels appearing at the head of each column.
AutoForm: Datasheet	Similar to the Tabular form, but in worksheet display format.
Chart Wizard	Displays data graphically.
PivotTable Wizard	Creates a form with an Excel PivotTable - an interactive table that can summarise a large number of data using the format and calculation methods specified by the user.

Access also allows you to design a form that contains another form. This type of form, called main/subform, allows data from related tables to be viewed at the same time.

Customising a Form:

You can customise a form by changing the appearance of text, data, and any other attributes. To have a look at some of these options, double click on Form1 to display the Customers form, then click the Design View button on the Toolbar.

What appears on your screen is shown below:

As you can see, a form in Design View is made up of boxes attached to a grid. Clicking at the County box, for example, causes markers to appear around it as shown above. When the mouse pointer is then placed within either the label box or data box, it changes to a hand which indicates that you can drag the box to a new position, as we have done above. This method moves both label and data boxes together.

If you look more closely at the markers around the label and data boxes, you will see that they are of different size, as shown below.

The larger ones are 'move' handles, while the smaller ones are 'size' handles. In the above example you can use the 'move' handles of either the label or the data box to move one independently of the other. The label box can also be sized. To size the data box, click on it so that the markers appear around it.

Boxes on a form can be made larger by simply pointing to the sizing handles and dragging them in the appropriate direction.

In addition to moving and enlarging label and data boxes, you can further customise a form using the various new buttons that appear on the Tool bar when in Design View, shown below in two tiers.

 Do try and experiment with moving and sizing label and data boxes and also increasing their font size. If you don't like the result, simply don't save it. Skills gained here will be used in the Report design section.

The Toolbox

The Toolbox can be used either to design a Form or Report from scratch (a task beyond the scope of this book), or to add controls to them, such as a Combo (drop-down) box. The function of each tool on the Toolbox is listed below.

Select Objects	Control Wizards
Label	Text Box
Option Group	Toggle Button
Option Button	Check Box
Combo Box	List Box
Command Button	Image
Unbound Object Frame	Bound Object Frame
Page Break	Tab Control
Subform/Subreport	Line
Rectangle	More Controls

As an example of using the Toolbox, let us assume that we would like to use a form to enter new data into our Invoices table, but with the ability of selecting the CustomerID field from a drop-down menu - a Combo box.

To achieve the above, execute the following steps:

- On the Database window first click the Forms tab followed by the **New** button.

- In the New Form dialogue box select the **Form Wizard** option, choose Invoices as the table on which to base the new Form, and press the **OK** button.

- In the second dialogue box, select all the fields from the Invoices table, and click the **Next** button.

- In the third dialogue box, select **Columnar** as the preferred form layout, and press **Next**.

- In the fourth dialogue box, select **Standard** as the preferred style for your form and press **Next**.

- In the fifth dialogue box, name your form 'Add Invoices', and press **Finish**. The following form is created and displayed on your screen.

- When the above form appears on the screen, click the Design View button on the Toolbar, and enlarge the Add Invoices form so that both the Header and Footer sections are visible on the form.

- Click the CustomerID field on the form, and delete both its Label and Data boxes by clicking each individually and pressing the <Del> key.

219

- Click the Combo Box on the Toolbox, and point and click at the area where the CustomerID field used to be on the form.

- In the subsequent dialogue boxes, select options which will cause the Combo Box to look up the values from the Customers table, and from the CustomerID field and store a selected value in the CustomerID field. Specify that the Combo Box should have the label Customer ID:.

- Move and size both the Label and Data boxes of the Combo box into the position shown below.

⊞ Add Invoices : Form		_ □ ×
· 1 · 1 · 1 · 2 · 1 · 3 · 1 · 4 · 1 · 5 · 1 · 6 · 1 · 7 ·		
◀ Form Header		
◀ Detail		
Invoice No	InvoiceID	
Customer ID	CustomerID ▾	
Date	Date	
Amount	Amount	
Paid?	Paid?	
◀ Form Footer		

- Click the Form View button on the Toolbar, followed by the New Record button at the bottom of the Add Invoices form, both of which are shown below.

- The entry form should now look as follows:

From now on, whenever you want to add a new invoice to the Invoices table, use the Add Invoices form from the Database window, then click the New Record button on either the Toolbar or the Add Invoices form itself to display an empty form. Next, type in the relevant information in the appropriate data boxes on the form, but when you come to fill in the Customer ID field, click instead the down arrow against its data box to display the drop-down menu shown here. Select one of the existing customers on the list, and click the Next Record button at the bottom of the Add Invoices form.

Try the above procedure with the following details:

   AD9714   WEST   28/10/97   £140

then verify that indeed the information has been recorded by double-clicking the Invoices table on the Database window.

Using the Report Wizard

We will use the skills gained in manipulating Forms in Design View to produce an acceptable report created by the Report Wizard. To produce a report of the Unpaid Invoices query, do the following:

- Click the Reports tab on the Database window and then press the **Next** button.

- In the New Report dialogue box, select the **Report Wizard** option, and choose the 'Unpaid Invoices' as the query where the object's data will come from, and press **OK**.

- Select all the fields (except for the Paid? field) which are to appear on your report and click the **Next** button.

- Select the InvoiceID field as the sort field, and accept all subsequent default settings. Call the report 'Unpaid Invoices Report'. The report is created for you as follows:

Unpaid Invoices Report

Invoice No	Order ID	Amount	Name	Contact	Phone
AD9701	97085VOR	£120.84	VORTEX Co. Ltd	Brian Storm	01776-223344
AD9703	97099BAR	£99.32	BARROWS Associ	Mandy Brown	01554-664422
AD9704	97002STO	£55.98	STONEAGE Ltd	Mike Irons	01765-234567
AD9705	97006PAR	£180.22	PARKWAY Gravel	James Stone	01534-987654
AD9706	97010WES	£68.52	WESTWOOD Ltd	Mary Slim	01234-667755
AD9707	97018GLO	£111.56	GLOWORM Ltd	Peter Summers	01432-746523
AD9709	97029WOR	£35.87	WORMGLAZE Ltd	Richard Glazer	01123-654321
AD9710	97039EAL	£58.95	EALING Engines D	Trevor Miles	01336-010107
AD9711	97045HIR	£290.00	HIRE Service Equi	Nicole Webb	01875-558822
AD9712	97051EUR	£150.00	EUROBASE Co. Lt	Sarah Star	01736-098765
AD9713	97097AVO	£135.00	AVON Constructio	John Waters	01657-113355
AD9713	97064AVO	£135.00	AVON Constructio	John Waters	01657-113355

Obviously this report is not quite acceptable. The problem is mainly the fact that all text fields are left justified within their columns, while numerical fields are right justified.

What we need to do is display it in Design View so that we can change the position of the numeric fields. To do this, double-click the Unpaid Invoices Report in the Database window to display it on screen, then click the Design View icon on the Toolbar which displays the Report as follows:

Use the mouse to move the Amount data box to the left, and then right justify the text in the Amount label and data boxes and make them smaller, as shown below.

The corresponding report is now as follows:

Unpaid Invoices Report

Invoice No	Order ID	Amount	Name	Contact	Phone
AD9701	97085VOR	£120.84	VORTEX Co. Ltd	Brian Storm	01776-223344
AD9703	97099BAR	£99.32	BARROWS Associate	Mandy Brown	01554-664422
AD9704	97002STO	£55.98	STONEAGE Ltd	Mike Irons	01765-234567
AD9705	97006PAR	£180.22	PARKWAY Gravel	James Stone	01534-987654
AD9706	97010WES	£88.52	WESTWOOD Ltd	Mary Slim	01234-667755
AD9707	97018GLO	£111.56	GLOWORM Ltd	Peter Summers	01432-746523
AD9709	97029WOR	£35.87	WORMGLAZE Ltd	Richard Glazer	01123-654321
AD9710	97039EAL	£58.95	EALING Engines Desi	Trevor Miles	01336-010107
AD9711	97045HIR	£290.00	HIRE Service Equipm	Nicole Webb	01875-558822
AD9712	97051EUR	£150.00	EUROBASE Co. Ltd	Sarah Star	01736-098765
AD9713	97097AVO	£135.00	AVON Construction	John Waters	01657-113355
AD9713	97064AVO	£135.00	AVON Construction	John Waters	01657-113355

This layout is obviously far more acceptable than that of the original report created by the Report Wizard.

* * *

We hope we have covered enough features of the program in this book to give you the foundations needed to make you want to explore Access more fully by yourself.

However, if you would prefer to be guided through additional topics, such as the use of functions in criteria, how to create Parameter, Crosstab, and Action queries, and how to use Masking and Filtering data, then may we suggest you look up the later chapters of the book *MS Access 97 one step at a time* (BP430), also published by BERNARD BABANI (publishing) Ltd.

* * *

15. SHARING INFORMATION

You can link or embed all or part of an existing file created either in an Office application or in any other application that supports Object Linking and Embedding (OLE). However, if an application does not support OLE, then you must use the copy/cut and paste commands to copy or move information from one application to another.

In general, you copy, move, link, embed, or hyperlink information depending on the imposed situation, as follows:

Imposed Situation	Method to Adopt
Inserted information will not need updating, or Application does not support OLE.	Copy or move
Inserted information needs to be automatically updated in the destination file as changes are made to the data in the source file, or Source file will always be available and you want to minimise the size of the destination file, or Source file is to be shared amongst several users.	Link
Inserted information might need to be updated but source file might not be always accessible, or Destination files needs to be edited without having these changes reflected in the source file.	Embed
To jump to a location in a document or Web page, or to a file that was created in a different program.	Hyperlink

Copying or Moving Information

To copy or move information between programs running under Windows, such as Microsoft applications, is extremely easy. To move information, use the drag and drop facility, while to copy information, use the **Edit, Copy** and **Edit, Paste** commands.

To illustrate the technique, we will copy the file **Project 3.xls** created in Excel into Word. We will consider the following two possibilities:

Source File Available without Application:

Let us assume that you only have the source file **Project 3.xls** on disc, but not the application that created it (that is you don't have Excel). In such a situation, you can only copy the contents of the whole file to the destination (in our case Word). To achieve this, do the following:

- Start Word and minimise it on the Taskbar.

- Use My Computer (or Explorer) to locate the file whose contents you want to copy into Word.

- Click the filename that you want to copy, hold the mouse button down and point to Word on the Taskbar until the application opens.

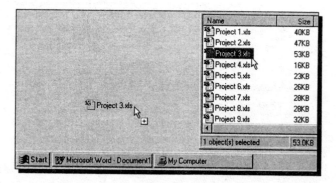

- While still holding the mouse button down, move the mouse pointer into Word's open document to the exact point where you would like to insert the contents of **Project 3.xls**.

- Release the mouse button to place the contents of **Project 3.xls** into Word at that point.

PROJECT ANALYSIS: ADEPT CONSULTANTS LTD

	Jan	Feb	Mar	1st Quarter
Income	£ 14,000.00	£15,000.00	£ 16,000.00	£ 45,000.00
Costs:				
Wages	£ 2,000.00	£ 3,000.00	£ 4,000.00	£ 9,000.00
Travel	£ 400.00	£ 500.00	£ 600.00	£ 1,500.00
Rent	£ 300.00	£ 300.00	£ 300.00	£ 900.00
Heat/Light	£ 150.00	£ 200.00	£ 130.00	£ 480.00
Phone/Fax	£ 250.00	£ 300.00	£ 350.00	£ 900.00
Adverts	£ 1,100.00	£ 1,200.00	£ 1,300.00	£ 3,600.00
Total Costs	£ 4,200.00	£ 5,500.00	£ 6,680.00	£ 16,380.00
Profit	£ 9,800.00	£ 9,500.00	£ 9,320.00	£ 28,620.00
Cumulative	£ 9,800.00	£19,300.00	£ 28,620.00	

Source File and Application Available:

Assuming that you have both the file and the application that created it on your computer, you can copy all or part of the contents of the source file to the destination file. To achieve this, do the following:

- Start Excel and open **Project 3.xls**.

- Highlight as much information as you would like to copy and click the copy icon on the Toolbar.

- Start Word and click the Paste icon on the Toolbar.

Object Linking and Embedding

Object Linking is copying information from one file (the source file) to another file (the destination file) and maintaining a connection between the two files. When information in the source file is changed, then the information in the destination file is automatically updated. Linked data is stored in the source file, while the file into which you place the data stores only the location of the source and displays a representation of the linked data.

For example, you would use Object Linking if you would want an Excel chart included in, say, a Word document to be updated whenever you changed the information used to create the chart in the first place within Excel. In such a case, the Excel worksheet containing the chart would be referred to as the source file, while the Word document would be referred to as the destination file.

Object Embedding is inserting information created in one file (the source file) into another file (the container file). After such information has been embedded, the object becomes part of the container file. When you double-click an embedded object, it opens in the application in which it was created in the first place. You can then edit it in place, and the original object in the source application remains unchanged.

Thus, the main differences between linking and embedding are where the data is stored and how it is updated after you place it in your file. Linking saves you disc space as only one copy of the linked object is kept on disc. Embedding a logo chosen for your headed paper, saves the logo with every saved letter!

In what follows, we will discuss how you can link or embed either an entire file or selected information from an existing file, and how you can edit an embedded object. Furthermore, we will examine how to mail merge a letter written in Word with a list created either in Access, Excel, Outlook, or even Word itself.

Embedding a New Object:

To embed a new object into an application, do the following:

- Open the container file, say Word, and click where you want to embed the new object.

- Use the **Insert, Picture** command, to display the additional drop-down menu, shown below.

- From this last drop-down menu action **Clip Art**, click the type of object you want to create, and press **OK**.

As an example, we selected **Clip Art** (you could select a different option) which opens the Microsoft Clip Gallery from which we selected the object shown here. Pressing the **Insert** button on the displayed Clip Gallery dialogue box, embeds the selected object within Word. We used the Draw application to add the ball in front of the cat. Double-clicking on such an embedded object, opens up the original application.

Another way of embedding objects is to use the **Insert, Object** command, which opens the Object dialogue box. In this, you have the option of creating 'New' objects, or creating objects from 'File'. Note that only applications that are installed on your computer and support OLE appear in the **Object Type** box.

Linking or Embedding an Existing File:

To embed an existing file in its entirety into another application, do the following:

- Open the container file, say Word, and click where you want to embed the file.

- Use the **Insert, Object** command, to open the Object dialogue box, shown below, when the **Create from File** tab is clicked.

To locate the file you want to link or embed, click **Browse**, and then select the options you want.

- In the **File Name** box, type the name of the file you want to link or embed.

- To maintain a link to the original file, check the **Link to File** box.

Note: To insert graphics files, use the **Insert, Picture, From File** command instead of the **Insert, Object** command. This displays the Insert Picture dialogue box which allows you to specify within the **Look in** box the folder and file you want to insert.

Linking or Embedding Selected Information:

To link or embed selected information from an existing file created in one application into another, do the following:

- Select the information in the source file you want to link or embed.

- Use the **Edit, Copy** command to copy the selected information to the Clipboard.

- Switch to the container file or document in which you want to place the information, and then click where you want the information to appear.

- Use the **Edit, Paste Special** command to open the following dialogue box:

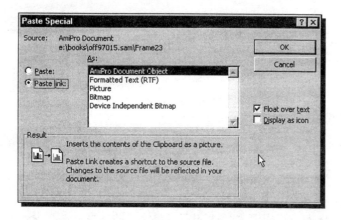

- To link the information, click the **Paste Link** radio button, or to embed the information, click the **Paste** radio button. In the **As** box, click the item with the word 'Object' in its name. For example, if you copied the information from an AmiPro document, as we have for this example, the AmiPro Document Object appears in the **As** box. Select this object and press **OK**.

232

Linking or Embedding into Access:

When you link or embed an object in a Microsoft Access form or report, the object is displayed in an object frame. To illustrate this point, start Access, select the Forms tab, and open Form1, which we created in Chapter 11. Then do the following:

- Switch to Design View, then use the **Insert, Object** command which displays the Insert Object dialogue box.

- Select the source application from the **Object Type** list (we have selected the Microsoft ClipArt Gallery), and press **OK**.

- Select the object and press **Insert**. This inserts the object into an unbound frame.

If the object you are embedding is from an Access table, use a bound object frame.

Editing an Embedded Object:

If the application in which you created an embedded object is installed on your computer, double-click the object to open it for editing. Some applications start the original application in a separate window and then open the object for editing, while other applications temporarily replace the menus and toolbars in the current application so that you can edit the embedded object in place, without switching to another window.

To edit an embedded object which was inserted into a Microsoft Access form or report, first switch to Design View, then double-click the object to open the application on which it was created.

If the application in which an embedded object was created is not installed on your computer, convert the object to the file format of an application you do have. For example, if your Word document contains an embedded Microsoft Works Spreadsheet object and you do not have Works, you can convert the object to an Excel Workbook format and edit it in Excel.

Some embedded objects, such as sound and video clips, when double-clicked start playing their contents, instead of opening an application for editing. To illustrate this, copy the Goodtime video icon from its folder in the Windows 95 CD into Word using the **Insert, Object** command (click the Create from File tab

and the Display as icon box on the displayed dialogue box), and Browse to the required icon. Double-clicking such an icon, starts the video.

To edit one of these objects, select it and use the **Edit, {Video Clip} Object, Edit** command. What appears within the curly brackets here depends on the selected object; video clip in this case.

234

Hypertext Links

Word publications (these are documents that contain hyperlinks to other locations) or Web pages, that others read online are made more interesting by inserting hyperlinks to other items. A hyperlink causes a jump to another location in the current document or Web page, to a different Word document or Web page, or to a file that was created in a different program. You can, for example, jump from a Word document to an Excel worksheet or to a PowerPoint slide to see more detail.

A hyperlink is represented by a 'hot' image or by display text (which is often blue and underlined) that you click to jump to a different location. To insert a hyperlink into Word files and Web pages, select the display text or image, and either use the **Insert, Hyperlink** command or click the Insert Hyperlink icon on the Toolbar. Either action opens a dialogue box which allows you to browse for the destination address.

To illustrate the procedure, start Word, open the **Pcusers 4** memo, and highlight the word 'Explorer' to be found towards the end of it. Next, click the Hyperlink icon and locate the **explorer.exe** file (in the **Windows** folder) using the **Browse** button, as shown below.

Pressing the **OK** button, underlines the highlighted text and changes its colour to blue. Pointing to such a hyperlink, changes the mouse pointer to a hand, as shown here to the left, and left-clicking it, starts the Explorer. When you have finished using the Explorer, click the Back icon on the Toolbar, shown here to the right, for the program to return you automatically to the hyperlinked Word document.

If the location of the file you wanted to hyperlink to is incorrect, or you did not highlight the word to be used as the hyperlink, then errors will occur. If that is the case, place the insertion pointer within the hyperlink word (use the arrow keys to place the I-beam on the word), click the Insert Hyperlink icon again, and press the **Remove Link** button at the bottom left of the displayed dialogue box.

As a second example, let us add to the **Pcusers 4** memo the following lines:

Hyperlinks can be used for displaying additional information, such as an Excel sheet, or a PowerPoint slide.

and save the result as **Pcusers 5**. However, before you can use a range of cells in an Excel Workbook as your hyperlinked object, you must first name such a range. Therefore, start Excel, open the **Project 9** file and name the cell range A1:F14 in the Consolidation sheet as Year_Summary, using the **Insert, Name, Create** command (hyperlinked ranges work better if they have been named with a single word, hence the underscore in the chosen name). Next, save your changes to **Project 9** and exit Excel.

Finally, select the word 'sheet' in the Word document to use it as the hyperlink to **Project 9.xls** and type Year_Summary in the **Named location in file** field box. For the PowerPoint object, you could select the word 'slide' to use as the hyperlink to **Training 3.ppt**.

Mail Merging Lists

There are times when you may want to send the same basic letter to several different people, or companies. The easiest way to do this is with a Merge operation. Two files are prepared; a 'Data' file with the names and addresses, and a 'Form' file, containing the text and format of the letter. The two files are then merged together to produce a third file containing an individual letter to each party listed in the original data file.

Before creating a list of names and addresses for a mail merge, you need to select the Office application that is most suited to the task. For a mail merge, you can use a list you create in Access, Excel, Outlook, or Microsoft Word.

- For a long list in which you expect to add, change, or delete records, and for which you want a powerful sorting and searching capabilities to your disposal, you should use either Access or Excel, then specify the appropriate data file in the Word Mail Merge Helper (see below).

- To use the list of names and addresses in your Outlook Contact List, you select this list in the Word Mail Merge Helper.

- For a small to medium size list of names and addresses in which you do not expect to make many changes, you could elect to create a list in the Word Mail Merge Helper.

The Word Mail Merger Helper is a dialogue box in which you specify:

(a) whether you want to create form letters, labels, or print envelopes, (b) where your list of names and addresses (data) is to be found, and (c) what query options are to be applied to your data list before the merging process starts. These will be explained next with illustrated examples.

We will illustrate the merge procedure by using a memo created in Word (**Pcusers 1**) and a table which can be created in Word, or already exists either in an electronic book such as Outlook, in Excel or in an Access table such as Customers in **Adept 1**.

No matter which method you choose, first start Word and open the **Pcusers 1** memo (or your own letter), then provide two empty lines at the very top of the memo/letter by placing the insertion pointer at the beginning of the memo and pressing <Enter> twice. Then select these two empty lines and choose the Normal paragraph style.

Next, select **Tools, Mail Merge** which displays the Mail Merge Helper dialogue box shown below.

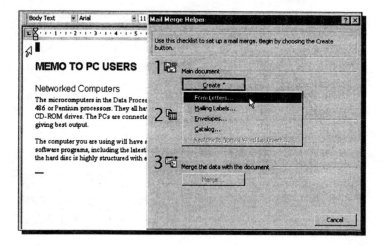

In this box, you define in three successive steps:

1. The document to be used,

2. The source of your data, and

3. The merging of the two.

Start by clicking the **Create** button, select the **Form Letters** option, and click the **Active Window** button.

Next, click the **Get Data** button which causes a drop-down menu to display, shown below.

It is from this menu that you can select either to create your data source (the list of addresses) in Word, open (or import) an existing list of addresses which might be found in either Word, Excel, Access, etc., or use a list of contacts in an electronic address book such as Outlook.

In what follows, we will examine each of these options (in the same order as the list in the above drop-down menu). You can, of course, skip the Create an Address List in Word section, if you already have an existing data list.

Creating an Address List in Word:

Selecting the **Create Data Source** menu option, displays the following dialogue box.

As you can see, Word provides commonly used field names for your address list. Unwanted field names can be deleted from the list by selecting them and pressing the **Remove Field Name** button. To add your own field name, type it in the **Field Name** box and press the **Add Field Name** button. The **Move** buttons to the right of the list can be used to move a selected field in the list to the top or bottom of the list by pressing the up-arrow or down-arrow, respectively.

Having compiled the required field names for your list, pressing the **OK** button, displays a Save As dialogue box, in which you can name your data list, say **Address**. Word automatically adds the file extension **.doc**, and displays the following warning dialogue box which allows you to either edit the data source or the main document.

Press the **Edit Data Source** button if you want to create or edit your data list. Doing so displays the following Data Form dialogue box.

Here you can create a new data list or edit an existing one. We have typed in one fictitious entry in order to demonstrate the process, but we have not attempted to change the field names provided in any way whatsoever.

Having created a Word data list, added to one or edited one, pressing **OK** saves your changes to the already existing filename.

What follows is common to all existing data files, no matter in which application you chose to create it.

Getting an Address List:

If you have not done so already, open the letter you want to mail merge, place the cursor in the position you want the address to appear, and select **Tools, Mail Merge** in Word. Then press the **Create** button in the Mail Merge Helper and choose **Form Letters**, **Active Window**.

Next, click the **Get Data** button (the 2nd step in the Mail Merge Helper) which causes a drop-down menu, shown here, to display.

Select the **Open Data Source** option, and in the displayed dialogue box, select the drive, and click the down-arrow on the **List Files of Type** box. From here you can choose the type of file that holds your address list, which could be one created in Word or a text editor (or exported in that form from another application), or an Access or Excel file.

For our example we chose the **MS Access Database** type of file, which lists the databases on the specified drive and path. Next, select the database that holds your address data (in this case **Adept 1.mdb**) and click the **Open** button. Access is then loaded and the tables within the selected database are listed, as shown below.

Microsoft Access then asks you to choose the Table that contains your data. In this case, select Customers and click the **OK** button.

Microsoft Word now displays a warning message, shown overleaf, to the effect that no merge fields have been found on your document.

Don't worry about this, as we will rectify this omission, as follows:

- Click the **Edit Main Document** button on the above warning box which displays your document with an additional toolbar below the Formatting bar, as follows:

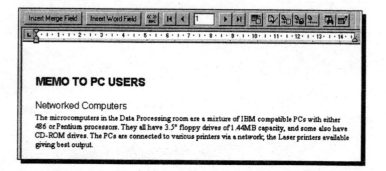

- Click the **Insert Merge Field** button on the new toolbar. This displays the fields in your Customers table.

- Select in turn, Name, Address, Town, County, and Post_Code. The first three are placed on the document on separate lines (by pressing <Enter> after each selection), while the last two are placed on the same line, but separated by a space. Finally, type on a new line the letters FAO: plus a space, and place the Contact field against it.

The first few lines of your document should now look as follows:

```
Insert Merge Field | Insert Word Field | ABC | I◄ | ◄ | 1 | ► | ►I | ⬚ | ...

«Name»
«Address»
«Town»
«County» «Post_Code»
FAO: «Contact»
```

MEMO TO PC USERS

Networked Computers

The microcomputers in the Data Processing room are a mixture of IBM compatible PCs with either 486 or Pentium processors. They all have 3.5" floppy drives of 1.44MB capacity, and some also have CD-ROM drives. The PCs are connected to various printers via a network; the Laser printers available giving best output.

- Click the View Merged Data icon, shown to the right, to see your merged data. Clicking this icon once more, returns you to the screen above so that you can edit your work, or add merge fields.

- Click either the Merge to New Document icon or the Merge to Printer icon to create a new merged document to file or send the merged document to the printer.

That's all there is to it. You will possibly find it takes as little time to do, as it did to read about it!

APPENDIX - GLOSSARY OF TERMS

Application
: Software (program) designed to carry out a certain activity, such as word processing.

Association
: An identification of a filename extension to a program. This lets Windows open the program when its files are selected.

ASCII
: A binary code representation of a character set. The name stands for 'American Standard Code for Information Interchange'.

Backup
: To make a back-up copy of a file or a disc for safe-keeping.

Bit
: A binary digit; the smallest unit of information that can be stored, either as 1 or as 0 (zero).

Bitmap
: A technique for managing the image displayed on a computer screen.

Browse
: A button in some dialogue boxes that lets you view a list of files and folders before you make a selection.

Buffer
: RAM memory allocated to store data being read from disc.

Byte
: A grouping of binary digits (0 or 1) which represent information.

Cache	An area of memory, or disc space, reserved for data, which speeds up down-loading.
Card	A removable printed-circuit board that is plugged into a computer expansion slot.
CD-ROM drive	A device which when in-stalled on your PC, allows the use of CDs.
Cell	The intersection of a column and row in a spreadsheet, or a table, which can hold an expression, a label or a number.
Check box	A small box in a dialogue box that can be selected ($\checkmark$), or cleared (empty).
Click	To quickly press and re-lease a mouse button.
Client	A computer that has access to services over a computer network. The computer pro-viding the services is a server.
Client application	A Windows application that can accept linked, or em-bedded, objects.
Clipboard	A temporary storage area of memory, where text and graphics are stored with the cut and copy actions.
Close	To remove a dialogue box or window, or to exit a pro-gram.

Command	An instruction given to a computer to carry out a particular action.
Configuration	A general purpose term referring to the way you have your computer set up.
CPU	The Central Processing Unit; the main chip that executes all instructions entered into a computer.
Cursor	The blinking line indicating where the next input can be entered.
Database	A collection of related information or data, organised for a specific theme in one or more tables.
DDE	Dynamic data exchange - a process that enables you to exchange data between two or more Windows programs.
Dial-up connection	A popular form of Internet connection for the home user, over standard telephone lines.
Default	The command, device or option automatically chosen by the system.
Desktop	The Windows screen working background, on which you place icons, folders, etc.
Device driver	A special file that must be loaded into memory for Windows to be able to address a specific procedure or hardware device.

Device name	A logical name used by the operating system to identify a device, such as LPT1 or COM1 for the parallel or serial printer.
Dialogue box	A window displayed on the screen to allow the user to enter information.
Dimmed	Unavailable menu options shown in a different colour.
Disc	A device on which you can store programs and data.
Disc file	A collection of program code, or data, that is stored on disc under a given name.
Document	A file produced by an application program.
Domain	A group of devices, servers and PCs on a network.
DOS	Disc Operating System; a collection of small specialised programs that allow interaction between user and computer.
Double-click	To quickly press and release a mouse button twice.
Download	To transfer to your computer a file, or data, from another computer.
DPI	Dots Per Inch; a resolution standard for laser printers.
Drag	To press and hold down the left mouse button while moving the mouse, to move an object on the screen.

Drive name	The letter (followed by a colon) which identifies a floppy disc drive, a hard disc drive, or a CD-ROM drive.
Embedded object	Information in a document that is 'copied' from its source application. Selecting the object opens the creating application from within the document.
Field	A single column of information of the same type.
File	The name given to an area on disc containing a program or data.
File extension	The optional three-letter suffix following the period in a filename. The extension is used to identify the filetype.
File list	A list of filenames contained in the active directory.
Filename	The name given to a file. In Windows 95 & 97 this can be up to 255 characters long.
Filespec	File specification made up of drive, path and filename.
Fixed disc	The hard disc of a computer.
Floppy disc	A removable disc on which information can be stored magnetically. The two main types are a 5¼" flexible disc, and a 3½" stiff disc.

Folder	An area on disc where information relating to a group of files is kept.
Font	A graphic design representing a set of characters, numbers and symbols.
Formatting	The process of preparing a disc so that it can store information.
FTP	File Transfer Protocol. The procedure for connecting to a remote computer and transferring files back to your local computer.
Function	A built-in formula which performs specific calculations in a spreadsheet or database cell.
Function key	One of the series of 10 or 12 keys marked with the letter F and a numeral, used for specific operations.
Graphics card	A device that controls the display on the monitor and other allied functions.
GUI	A Graphic User Interface, such as Windows, which uses visual displays to eliminate the need for typing commands.
Hardcopy	Output on paper.
Hard disc	A device built into the computer for holding programs and data. It is sometimes referred to as a fixed disc.

Hardware	The equipment that makes up a computer system, excluding the programs or software.
Help	A Windows system that gives you instructions and additional information.
Highlight	The change to a reverse-video appearance when a menu item or area of text is selected.
Home Page	The document displayed when you first open your Web browser, or the first document you come to at a Web site.
Host	A computer acting as an information or communications server.
HTML	HyperText Markup Language; the format used in documents on the Web.
HTTP	HyperText Transport Protocol; the system used to link and transfer hypertext documents on the Web.
Hypermedia	Hypertext extended to include linked multi-media.
Hypertext	A system that allows documents to be cross-linked so that the reader can explore related links, or documents, by clicking on a highlighted word or symbol.
Icon	A small graphic image that represents a function or

	object. Clicking on an icon produces an action.
Insertion point	A flashing bar that shows where typed text will be entered into a document.
Interface	A device that allows you to connect a computer to its peripherals.
Internet	The global system of computer networks.
ISDN	Integrated Services Digital Network; a telecom standard using digital transmission technology to support voice, video, and data communications applications over regular telephone lines.
Key combination	When two or more keys are pressed simultaneously, such as <Ctrl+Esc>.
Kilobyte	(KB); 1024 bytes of information or storage space.
LAN	Local Area Network; PCs, workstations or minis sharing files and peripherals within the same site.
Linked object	A placeholder for an object inserted into a destination document.
Links	The hypertext connections between Web pages.
Local	A resource that is located on your computer, not linked to it over a network.
Log on	To gain access to a network.

Long filename	In Windows 95 & 97 the name given to a file can be up to 255 characters long.
MCI	Media Control Interface - a standard for files and multimedia devices.
Megabyte	(MB); 1024 kilobytes of information or storage space.
Megahertz	(MHz); Speed of processor in millions of cycles per second.
Memory	Part of computer consisting of storage elements organised into addressable locations that can hold data and instructions.
Menu	A list of available options in an application.
Menu bar	The horizontal bar that lists the names of menus.
Microprocessor	The calculating chip within a computer.
MIDI	Musical Instrument Digital Interface - enables devices to transmit and receive sound and music messages.
MIME	Multipurpose Internet Mail Extensions; a messaging standard that allows Internet users to exchange e-mail messages enhanced with graphics, video, and voice.
Monitor	The display device connected to your PC.

Mouse	A device used to manipulate a pointer around your display and activate a certain process by pressing a button.
Multimedia	The use of photographs, music and sound, and movie images in a presentation.
Multi-tasking	Performing more than one operation at the same time.
Network server	Central computer which stores files for several linked computers.
Operating System	A group of programs that translates your commands to the computer.
Password	A unique character string used to gain access to a network, or an application document.
PATH	The location of a file in the directory tree.
PCX	A standard file format used for bitmapped graphics.
Peripheral	Any device attached to a PC.
Pixel	A picture element on screen; the smallest element that can be independently assigned colour and intensity.
POP	Point of Presence; the location of an Internet service provider, where users dial to

	connect to the host computer.
Port	An input/output address through which your PC interacts with external devices.
Print queue	The list of print jobs waiting to be sent to a printer.
Program	A set of instructions which cause the computer to perform certain tasks.
Protocol	It defines the way in which data is transferred over a network.
Processor	The electronic device which performs calculations.
RAM	Random Access Memory. The micro's volatile memory. Data held in it is lost when power is switched off.
Record	A row of information in a table relating to a single entry and comprising one or more fields.
Resource	A directory, or printer, that can be shared over a network.
Right-click	To click and release the right mouse button, which often opens a context sensitive menu in a Windows application.
ROM	Read Only Memory. A PC's non-volatile memory. Data is written into this memory

	at manufacture and is not affected by power loss.
Screen saver	A display program that moves images on an inactive screen.
Scroll bar	A bar that appears at the right side or bottom edge of a window.
Search Engine	A program that helps users find information across the Internet.
Server	A networked computer that is used to share resources.
Shared resource	Any device, program or file that is available to network users.
Site	A server, or a collection of linked Web pages at a single location.
Software	The programs and instructions that control your PC.
Spreadsheet	An electronic page made of a matrix of rows and columns.
SVGA	Super Video Graphics Array; it has all the VGA modes but with 256 colours.
Swap file	An area of your hard disc used to store temporary operating files, also known as virtual memory.
Table	A two-dimensional structure in which data is stored, like in a speadsheet.

Tags	Formatting codes used in HTML documents, which indicate how parts of a document will appear when displayed.
TCP/IP	Transmission Control Protocol/Internet Protocol; combined protocols that perform the transfer of data between two computers.
Template	A file blank you can create to contain common text and formatting to use as a basis for new documents.
Text file	An unformatted file of text characters saved in ASCII format.
Tool	Microsoft Office application, such as the word processor or spreadsheet.
Toolbar	A bar containing icons giving quick access to commands.
Toggle	To turn an action on and off with the same switch.
TrueType fonts	Fonts that can be scaled to any size and print as they show on the screen.
URL	Uniform Resource Locator; the addressing system used on the Web, containing information about the method of access, the server to be accessed and the path of the file to be accessed.

User ID	A one word name used to identify a specific user of a specific computer or network - usually assigned by the system administrator.
Virtual machine	A logical computer that Windows 95 creates in memory.
Virtual memory	See swap file.
Volume label	An identifying label written to a disc when it is first formatted.
WAIS	Wide Area Information Service; a Net-wide system for looking up specific information in Internet databases.
Web	See World Wide Web.
Web Page	An HTML document that is accessible on the Web.
Wildcard character	A character that can be included in a filename to indicate any other character (?), or group of characters (*).
World Wide Web	A network of hypertext-based multimedia information servers. Web browsers, such as the Internet Explorer, can be used to view any information on the Web.
Zoom	Enlarged view focusing on a portion of the page so that you can see the fine details of your page layout.

INDEX

COMPANION DISCS TO BOOKS

COMPANION DISCS are available for most books written by the same author(s) and published by BERNARD BABANI (publishing) LTD, as listed at the front of this book (except for those marked with an asterisk). These books contain many pages of file/program listings. There is no reason why you should spend hours typing them into your computer, unless you wish to do so, or need the practice.

COMPANION DISCS come in 3½" format with all example listings.

ORDERING INSTRUCTIONS

To obtain your copy of a companion disc, fill in the order form below or a copy of it, enclose a cheque (payable to **P.R.M. Oliver**) or a postal order, and send it to the address below. Make sure you fill in your name and address and specify the book number and title in your order.

Book No.	Book Name	Unit Price	Total Price
BP		£3.50	
BP		£3.50	
BP		£3.50	
Name		Sub-total	£............
Address:		P & P (@ 45p/disc)	£............
		Total Due	£............

Send to: P.R.M. Oliver, CSM, Pool, Redruth, Cornwall, TR15 3SE

PLEASE NOTE

The author(s) are fully responsible for providing this Companion Disc service. The publishers of this book accept no responsibility for the supply, quality, or magnetic contents of the disc, or in respect of any damage, or injury that might be suffered or caused by its use.